John O´Hanlon

The life and works of Saint Aengussius Hagiographus

or Saint Aengus the Culdee, bishop and abbot at Clonenagh and Dysartenos,

Queen's County

John O´Hanlon

The life and works of Saint Aengussius Hagiographus
*or Saint Aengus the Culdee, bishop and abbot at Clonenagh and Dysartenos,
Queen's County*

ISBN/EAN: 9783741158254

Manufactured in Europe, USA, Canada, Australia, Japa

Cover: Foto ©Thomas Meinert / pixelio.de

Manufactured and distributed by brebook publishing software
(www.brebook.com)

John O´Hanlon

The life and works of Saint Aengussius Hagiographus

THE

LIFE AND WORKS

OF

SAINT ÆNGUSSIUS HAGIOGRAPHUS.

THE

LIFE AND WORKS

OF

SAINT ÆNGUSSIUS HAGIOGRAPHUS

OR

SAINT ÆNGUS THE CULDEE,

𝕭ishop and 𝕬bbot

AT

CLONENAGH AND DYSARTENOS, QUEEN'S COUNTY.

BY THE

REV. JOHN O'HANLON.

"The learned in word shall find good things; and he that trusteth in the Lord is blessed.
"The wise in heart shall be called prudent: and he that is sweet in words shall attain to greater things.
"Knowledge is a fountain of life to him that possesseth it". — *Proverbs*, xvi. 20, 21, 22.

DUBLIN:
JOHN F. FOWLER, 3 CROW STREET,
DAME STREET
1868.

Dedication.

TO THE

Very Reverend Monsignore

PATRICK F. MORAN, D.D.,

Professor of Irish History

IN THE

CATHOLIC UNIVERSITY.

My Dear Dr. Moran,

You are already aware the following biographical notices, regarding a holy and learned Irishman, had been prepared to form the substance of a lecture. It was delivered in our city under the auspices and at the request of members constituting the charitable Society of St. John the Evangelist.* The object of this Religious Confraternity, being to promote the spiritual and corporal works of mercy, furnished motives sufficient to engage sympathy and coöperation. It was your good pleasure, with the present change of title, form, notes, and emendations, which

---

* On the 10th of September, 1858, in Alderman Crotty's Great Rooms, Christ Church Place. The original title of this Lecture was "The Life, Labours, and Learning of Ængus the Culdee, Irish Monk and Author of the Eighth Century".

met your kind approval, to wish a subsequent publication, in the IRISH ECCLESIASTICAL RECORD. Having
appeared in successive numbers of that most useful
and erudite periodical, owing so much of its interest
and value to your enlightened zeal and literary
ability, I have now ventured to reproduce this
memoir as a separate issue, and without material
alteration. I am very sensible of its many imperfec-
tions, and I feel altogether assured, that future historic investigators will be able to correct the writer's
various oversights and inaccuracies. However, it
must be admitted, Irish Hagiology presents a difficult
field in which to labour ; nor are its fruits yet sufficiently ripe for the harvest.

To no other person than yourself could the writer
more appropriately dedicate this little biographical
tract. He might indeed desire to render it much
more worthy of your acceptance, and much less
liable to the fair strictures of a candid criticism. It
is offered, however, as an humble tribute to real goodness of disposition and to distinguished talents, combined in just proportions. The services you have
rendered to Irish ecclesiastical history and biography
are destined, I fondly trust, to insure a prospective
increase. They have already deserved and obtained
national approbation.

With every sentiment of true esteem and respect,
my dear Dr. Moran, receive assurances of obligation
and regard from your faithful servant,

THE AUTHOR.

Dublin : SS. Michael and John,
Feast of the Immaculate Conception, 1868.

CONTENTS.

LIFE AND WORKS

ST. ÆNGUSIUS HAGIOGRAPHUS,

OR

ST. ÆNGUS THE CULDEE,

BISHOP AND ABBOT AT CLONENAGH AND DYSARTENOS, QUEEN'S
COUNTY.

I.—*Introduction.*—*Sources of biography to illustrate the acts of
St. Ængus.*—*His pedigree and early life.*—*He studies at the
monastery of Clonenagh.*—*Monastic training and learning.*

IF the life of every good man can be presented "to point a
moral and adorn a tale", some account regarding the labours,
learning, and life of a holy Irish monk, who flourished in the
eighth and ninth centuries, may claim attention and interest,
when brought before Irish readers. They serve to illustrate the
habits and usages of our early monasticism. Our regards cannot be lessened towards the subject of this biographical notice,
because he has deserved to rank among the host of Irish saints.
As a poet, too, his life abounds in the romance of reality. Much
could we desire to glean fuller particulars respecting him, and
to render his name and works more popularly known and appre-
ciated, than they have hitherto been. We can only offer some
brief biographical statements, and a necessarily imperfect analysis
regarding his valuable writings. The time must soon arrive,
when more satisfactory and learned efforts will make the venerable name of Ængus the Culdee be remembered and invoked,
by every pious and enlightened Irish Catholic.

The acts of this illustrious saint, known generally to Irish
scholars as Ængus the Hagiologist, have been published by

1

Colgan, at the 11th of March.[1] This latter researchful writer doubted not, that the life of Saint Æengus had been written at full length, and had been accessible, at a more remote period. But Colgan complains that this life was not available, at the time he had been engaged in publishing the acts of our Irish saints. However, the virtues of Æengus have been specially recorded, by some old writer, who prefixes an argument or an introduction to this saint's existing writings. Another Irish poet, likewise bearing the name of Æengus, has celebrated the Culdee's praises in certain verses, sufficiently indicative of great antiquity.[2]

Æengus the Culdee, sometimes named Æengusius Hagiographus, or Æeneas, is said to have been descended from Coelbach, king of Ireland.[3] The name of his father was Æengavan, called in Harris' *Ware*[4] Oengobhan, the son of Oblein, the son of Fidhraus, according to a genealogy made out for him in our Martyrologies.[5] He was sprung from the royal race of the Dalara-

---

[1] See Colgan's *Acta Sanctorum Hiberniae*, xi. *Martii. Vita Æengussii*, pp. 579 to 583.

[2] Colgan's *Acta Sanctorum Hiberniae*, xi. *Martii. Vita S. Æengussii*, cap. ii. p. 579. In note 5, p. 582, Colgan remarks, the author of this metrical life, in the penultimate verse of his panegyric on the saint, prays that he may enjoy with his namesake the bliss of eternal life. He extols St. Æengus with surpassing encomiums, stating that the saint was often engaged in colloquies with celestial spirits. He styles St. Æengus the Sun of Western Europe. On account of those things related regarding the studies of our saint in his youthful days, his daily and wonderful exercises, his rare humility and austerity, the day of his death, being *feria sexta*, the place of his burial, and such like notices, Colgan is under an impression, that the writer must have been a friend of St. Æengus, and have lived contemporaneously with him. Wherefore, owing to the concurrences of time, neighbourhood, and great erudition, it is supposed, that the writer had been no other than Æengus, Abbot of Cluain-fearta-Molua, who died in the year 858. See O'Donovan's *Annals of the Four Masters*, vol. i. pp. 492, 493. Colgan says, from the metrical panegyric, and the scholiast who wrote a preface to the Festilogy of Æengus, he derived all his materials for the life of this saint. A few particulars only are excepted, and these were drawn from other sources. See Colgan's *Acta Sanctorum Hiberniae*, xi. *Martii*, n. 5, p. 582.

[3] The following is St. Æengus' pedigree, as contained in a preface to his *Félire*, in the *Leabhar Breac*, R. I. A., Dublin: "Aengus, the son of *Oengoba*, son of *Oblen*, son of *Fidru*, son of *Diarmuit*, son of *Ainmire*, son of *Cellar*, son of *Oengus*, son of *Natsluagh*, son of *Caelbad* [of the Rudrician or Ultonian race, who was monarch of Erinn, and was slain, A.D. 357], son of *Crumbadrai*, son of *Eochaidh Cobai*". See Professor Eugene O'Curry's *Lectures on the Manuscript Materials of Ancient Irish History*, Lect. xvii. p. 363, and *Appendix*, No. cxi. p. 609.

[4] Vol. ii. *The Writers of Ireland*. Book i. p. 51.

[5] Such is an account left us by the anonymous scholiast on the Festilogium of Aengus, and to whom allusion has been made, as also in the *Sanctilogium Genealogicum*, cap. 23, where his genealogy is given in these words: " *S. Æengussius filius Æengavani, F. Hoblenii, F. Fidrai, F. Diermitii, F. Anmirechi, F. Cellarii, F. Æengussii, F' Natsluagii, F. Coelbadii, F. Crunnii Badhrai, F. Eochadii Cobhae, F. Lugadii, F. Rossii, F. Imchadii, F. Fethlemidii, F. Cassii, F. Fiach Aradii, a quo Dalaradiorum familia nominatur*". See Colgan's *Acta Sanctorum Hiberniae*, xi. *Martii. Vita S Æengussii*, nn. 1 et 3 p. 582.

dians in Ulster,[1] and he was born in Ireland, about the middle of the eighth century. Almost from infancy, he deserved the appellation *Culdee*,[2] or worshipper of God, which surname he afterwards bore. From the dawning perceptions of childhood, he felt an earnest desire of devoting himself to a religious life. He practised mortification to an extraordinary degree, even in his youth; and he conceived most exalted ideas of Christian perfection, the attainment of which was an object, ever uppermost in his mind.

About this time, the great monastery of Clonenagh, in Ossory, under direction of the saintly Abbot Malathgenius,[3] enjoyed a high reputation, both for the number and sanctity of its inmates. Ængus preferred his suit for admission within its enclosure, and his request was favourably received. But his early noviciate, in the exercise of all virtues, had preceded the care bestowed by that holy abbot, on his youthful disciple. His daily progress in the paths of Christian sanctity, and his advancement in sacred learning, were aided by application and capacity, to such an extraordinary degree, that in a short time he bore the reputation of being one among the most sanctified and erudite men, of whom Ireland could then boast.

An ingenious and a distinguished French writer,[4] capable from his peculiar line of study to pronounce opinions on this subject, has ably vindicated the progress made in sacred learning

---

[1] Colgan's *Acta Sanctorum Hiberniae, xi. Martii. ; Vita S. Ængussii*, cap. i. p. 579.

[2] " Toland pretends (*Nazarenus*, Letter ii. sect. 3) that the surname *Ceile De* given to Ængus indicated an office or particular sort of profession, and that he was one of that sort of clergymen, who have been afterwards called *Culdees*. But Ængus was a monk; whereas the Culdees, as will be seen elsewhere, were the secular canons of cathedral or collegiate churches, such as we call prebendaries. It is a palpable mistake to suppose, that they were a monastic order. The title, *Ceile De*, as applied to Ængus, had nothing to do with them; and it is more than probable that in his time there was not as yet any such institution as that of those so much talked of Culdees. Ængus's surname was peculiar to himself, unless it should be supposed that all that is said of his having been a monk, etc., is false. Many Irish names began with *Ceile, Cele*, or with the corresponding word *Gilta*, followed by that of our Saviour or some Saint"—Lanigan's *Ecclesiastical History of Ireland*, vol. iii. c. xx. § x. n. 96, p. 248.

[3] The death of " Maelaithgen, Abbot of Cluain-Eidhneach", occurred in the year 767. See O'Donovan's *Annals of the Four Masters*, vol. i. pp. 370, 371. The feast of St. Malathgenius is observed on the 21st. of October, and St. Ængus must have been his disciple before the year 767. For as that other Ængus, who wrote the eulogy of our Saint in elegant metre, has told us that Ængus the Culdee studied from boyhood in the monastery of Clonenagh, and afterwards, when he had been celebrated for his miracles, he lived in the monastery of Tallagh, before St. Melruan's death, A.D. 787. It is supposed, therefore, to follow, that he studied in the monastery of Clonenagh under the aforesaid abbot. See Colgan's *Acta Sanctorum Hiberniae, xi. Martii*, n. 4, p. 582.

[4] M. de la Villemarque, of the French Institute, has published a most interesting article on the Poetry of the Celtic Cloisters. It appeared in the November number of *Le Correspondant* for 1863.

and science among the pupils of our early schools. When the Celt became a Christian and a monk, his love of numbers still remained, and his conceptions becoming spiritualised by the aspirations after perfection, which he daily breathed heavenward, poetic inspiration was the happy result. Study, with manual labour, divided cloistral occupations, and through study this inspiration became fruitful. The saints of Ireland, intent only on making their disciples spiritual men, one day found to their surprise they had created poets. The genius of these poets was varied, as the crowd of strangers that thronged the schools. Their compositions may be reduced under the heads of didactic poetry, lyrical poetry, Amras or panegyrics, legends strictly so called, Felires or Festologies, visions, and navigations or voyages. All these have their special features of interest and edification. However, owing to various causes, facts were now and then changed into fictions. But M. de la Villemarque is far from agreeing with those, who consider romances regarding the saints as worthless. According to him, the portraits of saints simply underwent the fate of all heroes belonging to early ages; and yet, between the sacred and profane legends there exists a great difference. In what profane legend do we ever find an express caution to the reader, that, beside the literal and historical sense, there is also a spiritual meaning to be drawn from the narrative?[1] That delicate and sound morality which marks the legends of the Breton and Irish saints, has been specially dwelt on by a modern critic. For freshness, richness of invention, and national characteristics, no church has aught to compare with them. And all Celtic scholars will acknowledge this high degree of praise to be fully deserved.

Accounts which are given respecting the miracles and sanctity of Ængus, and the evidences of his learning that yet remain, are more than equalled by that profound humility which led him to form a most abject opinion regarding his own deserts. The manner in which he renounced this world and the applause of mankind, must deserve unbounded admiration, although it may fail to induce the imitation of all professing Christians. His mind was replenished with heavenly graces, and he was favoured with celestial visions. He combined the rare gifts of profound wisdom and singular zeal, in all his

---

[1] M. de la Villemarque shows that Dante fully realized this double nature of the ancient legends.

> " Ye of intellect,
> Sound and entire, mark well the lore conceal'd
> Under close texture of the mystic strain".
> *Inferno, IX.*, 62.—*Cary's Transl.*

actions and affections; while it would be a difficult question to decide, whether his virtues were greater than his miracles in sight of God and man. One thing, however, is certain, that the nobility of his descent was more than surpassed by the lustre of his virtues.

II.—*St. Ængus retires to Dysart Enos.—His austerities.—Repu-*
tation for sanctity.—He visits the Church of Coolbanagher.—
A vision of angels.—The purpose it evoked.

Some six or seven miles from Clonenagh, Ængus had built a cell[1] for himself. Thither he frequently retired, to put in practice, unknown and unnoticed, those rigorous observances which he followed. The locality of this cell hence derived its name, Dysartenos, or the desert of Ængus,[2] which it yet retains. A broken range of limestone hills, of romantic and rugged outline, probably suggested to him the idea of its suitableness as a place for seclusion and retreat. At the present day, the scenes of his retirement present an aspect of solitude and grandeur, the effect of which must have been considerably heightened in that early age.[3] An extensive tract of morass and bog now intervenes between the ruins of Clonenagh's old monastery and Dysart-

---

[1] That he built a cell for himself at Dysart Enos may be inferred, not only from the expression of Colgan, " coluit eremum", but also from a statement that he recited the first fifty psalms " in oratorio", and the second fifty, " sub diu juxta proceram arborem oratorio adjacentem". See *Acta Sanctorum Hiberniae, xi. Martii, Vita S. Aengussii,* cap. iii. p. 579.

[2] The anonymous scholiast, already mentioned, calls it *Disert Ænguis :* and the other Ængus, who wrote our saint's eulogy, writes it down as *Disert-Bethech.* He likewise indicates that it lay very near to Clonenagh. Colgan adds, " vel forte ab ipso non esse diversum, in quatenus ait in S. Ængussium esse in jam memorato deserto (et non addit quod non in Cluain-edhneach), et educatum et sepultum". Wherefore, Colgan thinks the Desert in question was identical with Cluain-edneach, or at least that Ængus perchance died and had been buried in the place first named. Our annals certainly show that a *Desertum Ængussii* differed from Cluain-edhneach. These record that Conn, son of Maelpadraig, Archinnech of Disert-Oenghusa and of Mungairit, died A.D. 1033. See Colgan's *Acta Sanctorum Hiberniae, xi. Martii,* n. 6, p. 582 ; and O'Donovan's *Annals of the Four Masters,* vol. ii. pp. 826, 827. In a note (y) *ibid.,* I am certain, Dr. O'Donovan fell into an error, by identifying the latter Disert-Aengusa with Dysart-Enos, in the Queen's county. I feel satisfied the Disert-Aengussa and Mungairit, already named, were both situated within the present county of Limerick. The former lay near Ballingarry, and the latter near Limerick city.

[3] Near the Dysart Hills, lies a beautiful demesne called Lamberton Park. Here, during the Wizard of the North's tour through Ireland in 1825, he was hospitably entertained by a former proprietor, the Right Hon. Judge Moore, as may be seen, by consulting Lockhart's *Life of Sir Walter Scott,* chap. lxiii. What Lockhart forgets to state, however, is yet traditionally remembered in this neighbourhood. Sir Walter is said to have expressed himself, as being highly gratified by the scenic beauty of all this surrounding locality ; and it must be allowed, few persons had truer perceptions of taste and judgment, in reference such matters.

enos. This moorland must have rendered access between both places, a matter of some difficulty to our saint. In this favourite retreat, we are told by his biographers, he was in the habit of making three hundred genuflections each day, and of reciting the entire Psalter. This latter office he divided into three separate portions: the first was said within the cell; the second under a spreading tree of large growth, that cast its branches over his rude habitation; and the third he repeated whilst tied by the neck to a stake, with half of his body plunged in a tub of cold water. Besides these extraordinary practices, he was continually employed in singing the praises of God, and in acquiring such an ascendancy over his passions, that to all save himself, Ængus seemed to be an angel concealed in human form.

Another and a learned authority has stated, that after leaving Clonenagh, St. Ængus travelled into Munster, and that he founded the church of Disert Aengusa, at a place situated near Ballingarry, in the present county of Limerick.[1] We are told also that the primitive belfry, or round tower of this church, yet remains. There are good reasons for believing, however, that the latter church must have had its name from some other saint, or person, named Ængus; for our saint is known to have settled not far from Clonenagh—in fact, so very near, that the localities Clonenagh and Dysartenos have been confounded by ancient scholiasts on his works.[2] Other circumstances, relating to his acts and incidents of his life, confirm our conclusions, that he lived, for some short time at least, in Dysartenos, a parish so denominated, near the celebrated Rock of Dunamase, and a few miles from Maryborough.

The fame of his sanctity diffused itself, to most distant parts of the country. Numbers flocked towards his retreat, to enjoy the pious conversation and exhortations of this holy anchorite, and to derive from his example and instructions those lessons of virtue which he could so well inculcate. Fearing the sugges-

---

[1] See Professor Eugene O'Curry's *Lectures on the Manuscript Materials of Ancient Irish History.* Lect xvii. p. 364.

[2] "All the country about *Cluainenach* for many miles, was, in the memory of men yet living, a great forest. * * * * *Desert Ængus* (though the name be now lost) was some part of this great wood".—Harris' *Ware,* vol. iii. *Writers of Ireland,* book i. pp. 51, 52, note D. Harris lived in the earlier part of the last century, when his principal works were published. He intimates, likewise, that the place of his birth was at or near Brittas, where his father, Captain Lieutenant Hopton Harris of the Militia, took part in an engagement, during the Jacobite and Williamite wars in 1691. See Walter Harris' *History of the Life and Reign of William the Third,* book ix. pp. 316, 317. Hence, we may take it for granted, this writer had a good local knowledge respecting Clonenagh and Disart Enos. But, because he did not advert to the possible identity of the later denomination with Desart Ængus, he thought this place where St. Ængus resided could not then be identified.

tions of vain-glory, and finding it a matter of utter impossibility to enjoy, in his present abode, that perfect seclusion desired, in the practice of his austerities and devotions, Ængus took the resolution of departing in a secret manner, towards some other place of retirement.

Before his departure, however, and on the route to his selected retreat, it was his intention to visit the church of Coolbanagher,[1] for the purpose of offering up prayers to that God, whom he so faithfully served. Whilst engaged in this exercise, a vision of angels appeared to him. These blessed spirits seemed to surround a particular tomb. Celestial songs were heard by him, at the same time, the ravishing harmony of which gave him a foretaste of canticles, entoned by the beatified in heaven. He noted the tomb thus distinguished, and immediately directed his steps to a priest serving the church. Ængus made inquiries regarding the name and character of the deceased. He soon learned that the occupant of the tomb in question had been in early life a warrior, who retired from the profession of arms and devoted himself to a life of penance. This soldier of Christ had closed a long life of holy and spiritual warfare, a few days before such event. Ængus was still more desirous to learn the practices, devotions, and penitential exercises of the soldier. His curiosity being gratified, he was unable to discover anything very unusual, in these his religious observances, with the exception of a practice he followed each morning and night, which was that of invoking the prayers of all saints, whose names occurred to his memory. From this relation given by the priest, the idea of composing a metrical hymn, in honour of

---

[1] The old church of Coolbanagher yet remains in a ruinous state, and its surrounding graveyard is now used as a place of burial. Tradition assigns to the building an early date of erection. There are two divisions in this church yet visible—most probably the nave and choir. A wall appears to have separated both, but a large pointed doorway afforded a communication. The nave, on the outside, measures thirty-two feet in length by twenty-two feet in breadth. The outside wall of the choir measures twenty-eight feet, in length, by sixteen feet, in breadth. The inside of the building is filled with loose stones and rubbish. A narrow low door, now stopped up with masonry, appears beneath an overshadowing mass of ivy, on the western gable; and a door seems to have been subsequently opened, on the southern side wall, probably, when the former one had been closed. A splayed window opened on either side of the nave. A splayed and ruinous east window formerly lighted the choir, the side walls of which are now nearly level with the ground. These are some descriptive particulars noticed during a visit to the spot, on the 10th of December, 1853. On that occasion, the writer took a pencil sketch of the old church ruins, as they appeared from the south-east side of the building. There are no tombs, at present, in the graveyard or church, but such as bear modern inscriptions. The old building is apparently of very great antiquity. It adjoins the ruins of Coolbanagher Castle, near the great Heath of Maryborough. In Sir Charles Coote's *Statistical Survey of the Queen's County*, we are simply informed that "at Coolbanagher are the ruins of a church and also of a castle". Chap. xi. § 4. p. 136.

all the saints, took possession of his mind.[1] This hymn he intended to repeat to his death, although his sincere humility deterred him from the immediate prosecution of his project. Ængus, we are told, judged himself unfitted for such a task, and feared that the praises of the saints might be commemorated in a manner, hardly suited to the dignity and importance of his subject.

III.—*St. Ængus proceeds to the Monastery of Tallagh.—Seeks admission there in guise of a servant.—Manual labour at agricultural operations.—His humility and mortifications.—An accident which befel him, and his miraculous cure.*

At this time St. Molruan presided over a great monastery on Tallagh Hill, in the present county of Dublin. Towards this religious house, our saint proceeded.[2] He appeared at the gate

---

[1] To this incident, allusion has been made by Thomas D'Arcy M'Gee, in that beautiful dirge, composed on the lamented death of his friend Eugene O'Curry:—

> " Let those who love and lose him most,
> In their great sorrow comfort find,
> Remembering how heaven's mighty host
> Were ever present to his mind;
> Descending on his grave at even,
> May they a radiant phalanx see—
> Such wondrous sight as once was given
> In vision to the rapt Culdee".

Instead of the buried person being called a "soldier", according to an account found in Professor O'Curry's *Lectures on the Manuscript Materials of Ancient Irish History*, he is said to have been "a poor old man, who formerly lived at the place. What good did he do? said Aengus. I saw no particular good by him, said the priest, but that his customary practice was to recount and invoke the saints of the world, as far as he could remember them, at his going to bed and getting up, in accordance with the custom of the old devotees. Ah! my God, said Aengus, he who would make a poetical composition in praise of the saints should doubtless have a high reward, when so much has been vouchsafed to the efforts of this old devotee! And Aengus then commenced his poem on the spot. He subsequently continued it gradually, and finished it as we have already seen". Lect. xvii. p. 365. According to the same learned authority, our saint commenced this poem, known as the Festology, at Cuil Bennchair in Offaly, continued it at Cluain Eidhnech, and finished it during his servitude at Tallagh. *Ibid.* If such be the case, it is probable St. Ængus left Dysartenos, and spent some time in his *alma mater* at Clonenagh, before he proceeded to Tallagh.

[2] In this *Report of the Census Commissioners of Ireland for the year* 1851, part v. vol. i., we find a most valuable annalistic reference to diseases and pestilences in this country from the earliest times to the present. In this able report, which does so much credit to the learning and research of Sir William Wilde, we find various accounts, which serve to furnish a derivation for Tallaght or Tamlacht. The Annals commence with the first recorded pestilence, or *Tamh*—namely, that which destroyed Parthalon's colony, and which is referred by the *Four Masters* to A.M. 2820, according to the long chronology of the Septuagint. The entry by those annalists is, "Nine thousand of Parthalon's people died in one week on Sean-Mhagh-Ealta-Edair—namely, five thou-

of this monastery, and begged admission amongst the members of its religious fraternity, in quality of lay brother, according to Colgan and Harris;[1] although Dr. Lanigan tells us, that such a title was unknown in religious houses before the eleventh century.[2] He studiously concealed both his name and that of the monastery, in which he had hitherto lived; for Ængus was well aware, that his fame had already extended to the institute of Tallaght, which was then in its infancy. Wherefore, he assumed a habit, calculated most effectually to disguise his real condition. He concealed the fact of his enrolment in the ecclesiastical order,

sand men and four thousand women. Whence is (named) Tamlacht Muintire Parthaloin"—"the place", adds Dr. Wilde, in his notice of the event, "now called Tallaght, near Dublin; and the tumuli of these early colonists, who died from sudden epidemic, can still be seen upon the hills in its vicinity. This is the first recorded pestilence in Ireland. The Irish word *Tamh* means an epidemic pestilence; and the term *Tamhleacht* (the plague monument), which frequently enters into topographical names in Ireland, signifies a place where a number of persons cut off by pestilence were interred together.—See Cormac's *Glossary MSS.* See also note by O'Donovan in his *Translation of the Annals of the Four Masters.* This destruction of the colony of Parthalon, which is said to have occurred in 'the old plain of the valley of the flocks', stretching between Ben Edair (Howth) and Tallaght, on which the city of Dublin now stands, is thus mentioned in the 'Book of Invasions', contained in the *Book of Leinster* (manuscript, Mr. Curry's translation.) 'In Sean-Magh-Etair Parthalon became extinct in a thousand men and four thousand women, of one week's mortality', or *Tamh.* This is the oldest manuscript account of that pestilence that we now possess; and in an ancient bardic poem in the *Book of Leinster*, it is said: 'Parthalon's people, to the number of nine thousand, died of *Tamh* in one week' ". Other authorities on the same subject are then cited, and among the rest the *Chronicon Scotorum MSS.*, as translated by Mr. Curry, where the following entry occurs:—" In one thousand five hundred and four (400 according to Eochaidh O'Flinn) from Parthalon's arrival in Ireland till the first mortality (*Duine-bhadh, i.e.*, human mortality) that came in Ireland after the Deluge; that is, the death by pestilence (*Tamh*) of Parthalon's people, which happened on Monday, in the calends of May, and continued till the Sunday following. It was from that mortality (*Duine-bhadh*) of Parthalon's people the name of the *Taimleachta* (the death or mortality place) of the men of Ireland is derived".

[1] Colgan says, he applied for admission, "inter conversos". *Acta Sanctorum Hiberniae, xi. Martii. Vita S. Ængussii*, cap. v. p. 581. Harris states that he was received "by the Abbot Maelruan, as a lay brother". Harris' *Ware*, vol. ii. *Writers of Ireland*, book i. p. 52.

[2] "Harris (*Writers* at *Ængus*) says that he was received as a lay-brother. Colgan indeed, from whom he took his account of Ængus, seems to have thought so; for he represents him as *conversus*, the term by which a lay brother is usually distinguished from a clerical one. But if this was Colgan's meaning, he was certainly mistaken; for the distinction between clerical and lay monks or brethren, as it is now understood, was not known in Ireland at that period, nor, it seems, any where until the eleventh century. (See Fleury, *Discours septieme sur l'Hist. Eccl.*, and *Instit. an Droit Eccl.*, part i. ch. 25.) In older times some monks, it is true, were raised more or less to the clerical ranks, and the number of such promotions appears to have increased with the course of ages; but there was not as yet any radical distinction of classes in the religious institutions, so as that one of them was perpetually debarred from any ecclesiastical promotion, and destined to toil in the fields and elsewhere as subordinate to the other, and, in fact, as servants of the clerical or higher class". *Ecclesiastical History of Ireland*, vol. iii. chap. xx. § x. n. 95, p. 247, 248.

and appeared as a serving man, seeking for service. This holy servant of Christ was permitted to prove his vocation for a religious life, by engaging in the most laborious and meanest offices, connected with the monastery. These duties, however, he most cheerfully executed, and he devoted unremitting attention to their most careful performance. He was principally employed at field labour, and in the farm-yard belonging to the monastery; for we are told, that with the sweat of his brow he was found as a reaper of corn during the harvest, that he bore the sheaves on his back to the barn, that he afterwards threshed out the grain, and winnowed chaff therefrom, placing what had been thus prepared in sacks. Like a beast of burden, he carried those sacks on his back, sometimes to the granary, and sometimes to the mill. This mill and a kiln, he had charge of by Melruan's orders.[1] During all these labours, this devout and humble brother found time to raise his heart and thoughts towards heaven. This ark of hidden wisdom considered himself, as only fitted to discharge the mean offices, to which of choice he subjected himself. These daily toils showed his complete self-abnegation, and his contempt for the opinion of worldlings. During his labours this humble monk was scantily clothed. His countenance was often disguised, owing to the combined effects of sweat and dust, which covered his features. But, he had neither the vanity nor inclination to appear well-looking in the presence of his brethren. Nor would he devote any time to the decoration of his person. He allowed the hair on his head to grow long, tangled and uncombed; the chaffy dust and straws of the field and barn, he would not even remove from his clothes. Thus Ængus conceived himself, as putting into practical operation the virtues of his monastic profession; for it was only by these means, he could induce worldlings to believe, that he was the most abject and vile of all creatures, having more the appearance of a monster, than of a human being. An extraordinary love of mortification was united with extatic flames of Divine love, in the soul of this great vessel of election; and hence, he merited the title of Kele-De,[2] which he obtained, and which may be rendered, "a lover of God". With an humble spirit, in a mortified body, a light radiated the interior of his soul. Yet this light was destined to escape from the close sanctuary, within which it had hitherto beamed.

[1] See, Professor Eugene O'Curry's *Lectures on the Manuscript Materials of Ancient Irish History.* Lect. xvii. p. 365. The author of this learned work declares, that he saw the ruins of this mill and kiln, in their primitive dimensions, and that only a few years have passed by, since these venerable relics have yielded to "the improving hand of modern progress".

[2] "Quae vox latine reddita Deicolam, seu Amadaeum designat". Colgan's *Acta Sanctorum Hibernia,* xi. Martii. *Vita S. Ængussii,* cap. v. p. 580.

Meantime, it may be well to relate, that the Almighty was pleased to reward the virtues of his servant, and by the testimony of a surprising miracle. For, at one time, whilst this holy monk was engaged in a neighbouring wood cutting down branches for the use of his monastery, it happened, that he held with the left hand a branch, which he wished to separate from the trunk of a tree, and the axe, grasped in his right hand, glanced from the object against which it had been directed. This incautious stroke resulted in severing the left hand from his body. We are told, the very birds, in the wood, by a sort of preternatural instinct, had formed an attachment towards St. Ængus, on account of his innocent demeanour. Perhaps, the holy man had often lightened his out-door labours, by chaunting the psalmody of the Church,—probably adapted to verses of his own composition. Those feathered warblers, the thrushes or blackbirds—so often celebrated in Ossianic song[1]—had made the dells and brakes around Glenasmoil and Tallagh resound with dulcet melody, while spring and summer breezes loaded the air with agreeable perfume from mountain herbs and shrubs. Their strains were often stilled, when more solemn and pathetic notes, from " a son of song", agreeably called forth the natural echoes, which resounded through wooded hill-sides and hollows, surrounding St. Melruan's monastery. Those songsters of the grove and thicket will rest with listening ear, and love to linger near any spot, where the humble field-labourer pours forth the unpremeditated lay, with a clear and modulated voice. If not disturbed, these woodland minstrels even desire human companionship and vocalism of a perfect character. We cannot doubt, the Christian's heart was naturally gentle and toned with refined feeling, while the poet's soul and senses were attuned to all the soft and sweet influences of wild scenery and its charming accessories. Sometimes, it is said, even ravens flap their wings with affright, when from a distance they scent human blood. A mysterious sympathy frequently unites irrational to rational creatures. At the moment this accident befel Ængus, birds flocked around, and by their screams and cries, seemed to bewail the pure and angelic man's misfortune. Full of confidence in the power and goodness of God, without hesitation, Ængus took up the hand which had been lopped off, and at once set it, in its proper place, at the extremity of his mutilated arm. Instantly, it adhered, and recovered its former power, as if no accident whatever had befallen him. Hereupon Ængus poured forth his soul, in praise and thanksgiving, to the great preserver of all creatures.[2]

[1] See Laoiche Fiannuicheachta, edited by John O'Daly, n. 1, p. 4. *Transactions of the Ossanic Society for the year* 1856, vol. iv.
[2] See Colgan's *Acta Sanctorum Hiberniae, xi. Martii. Vita S. Aengussii,* cap. vi. p. 580.

Our popular traditions, especially referring to the saints, often savour of exaggeration. The Irish people have loved and admired purity and holiness, while they have implicit faith in the sovereign power of God towards and over his elect. The foregoing miracle—one of the few miracles recorded about our saint, although he is said to have wrought many—may be classed with our *Legenda Sanctorum.* Probably, its rationale would accord better with the fact, that St. Ængus had almost chopped the left hand from his arm, but that he had immediately bandaged and united these members of his body, so nearly dissevered, and yet so fortunately preserved for future use. In the case of wounds, eminent surgeons allow, that very dangerous ones are often healed by prompt attention, and by a recuperative energy found in the human body itself. If a piece of flesh be totally cut away and soon after applied to the place whence taken, both parts will again unite. By the popular rumour, the cure of St. Ængus has been pronounced miraculous. However it had been effected, we cannot fail to recognize the Almighty's bounty towards a favoured servant, who was destined to effect still greater good, and acquire additional merits, before his day of deliverance from earth had arrived.

IV.—*The incident which first discovered St. Ængus to the Holy Abbot St. Melruan.—Friendship thenceforth existing between them.—Literary pursuits of our Saint.—Engages on the Felire or Festology.—Presents a copy of it to Fothadius the Canonist. —Probable date, origin, and object of the Felire.*

St. Ængus continued to exercise his usual austerities, and remained unknown to the monks and to the rest of mankind, for seven whole years. At length, an unusual occurrence betrayed the secret he seemed so anxious to conceal. Whilst Ængus was at work one day in the monastery barn, a scholar who had not thoroughly prepared his lesson, and who was in consequence afraid to appear in school, applied for admission and concealment, at least during that day. When Ængus learned the cause of this boy's uneasiness, he spoke kindly and with cheering assurances: pressing the child to his bosom, he contrived to lull the scholar to sleep. After some time, he was awakened, and desired to repeat his lesson.[1] He proceeded in the task,

[1] Dr. Lanigan undertakes to explain the circumstance of this boy's proficiency in his lesson, owing to the help he derived from Ængus. See, *Ecclesiastical History of Ireland,* vol. iii. chap. xx. § x. p. 246. At note 97 he adds: "It is thus, I think, that the anecdote related in Ængus' *Acts* ought to be understood. The boy's improvement is indeed stated as miraculous, and as a supernatural consequence of his having slept for awhile on the bosom of Ængus. But, it can be well accounted for without recurring to a miracle". *Ibid.,* p. 248.

repeated every word to the end, and this was done without
hesitation or difficulty. Ængus exacted from him a promise of
silence regarding these circumstances, and recommended him
immediately to seek his teacher. The latter, on examination of
his disciple, found him very well prepared on this day—an
occurrence of rare result in the boy's course of training. His
master, no less a personage than the Abbot, St. Melruan himself, insisted on learning the cause of his forwardness, at this
particular juncture. Awed by the Abbot's authority and earnest
manner, the boy revealed the circumstances of his case, as they
had actually occurred. By a sudden inspiration, a belief in the
identity of this monk with the missing Ængus of Dysartenos,
rushed upon the mind of the superior over the Tallaght community. He ran immediately to the barn, and embraced Aengus
with most tender affection, lavishing on him reproaches which
love and admiration could alone dictate. He was blamed for
the long-borne and humiliating, though willing, services rendered to the community, and for that false humility, which
deprived it of the learning and experience possessed by so
great a master of the spiritual life. Aengus fell on his knees, at
the feet of Abbot Melruan, and he begged and obtained pardon
for those faults, which merited loving reproaches. From that
time forward, they became bosom friends, and unconscious rivals
in that holy ambition, by which a true saint is ever prompted.[1]
  The literary labours, in which St. Ængus engaged, have
given him very great celebrity through after times; but in all
probability he had not then formed the most remote idea,
regarding this merited renown. His works are of exceeding
value, not only as having been composed, at a comparatively remote period; but, because the subjects on which they treat give
them a historical value and importance, of which ancient pieces
can rarely boast. Fiction is too often blended with fact, in
many such tracts, to the great prejudice of their authenticity.
Numerous saints, that adorned the early Irish Church, are named
in his writings, and are thus preserved, for the veneration of
posterity. While his own name has been exalted by his various
works, the country that gave him birth derives no small share
of renown from accounts he has left, respecting her beatified
children. Hence, we are enabled to estimate the services of
Ængus to sacred learning and literature, in a new light; for

The affectionate, kind, and patient teacher was probably exemplified in the
case of Ængus; and hence, the child might have been encouraged to greater
mental exercise by his instructions and the method he took in communicating
them.
  [1] Colgan's *Acta Sanctorum Hiberniae*, xi. Martii. *Vita S. Ængussii*, cap.
vii., viii., ix., p. 580.

happily, in him we have found a true saint to record the actions of his sanctified compatriots and predecessors.

No sooner had Ængus been called to fill a different sphere of life in the monastery, from that in which he had been at first exercised, than the unforgotten vision of angels seen in Coolbanagher Church, and the purpose it evoked, came with new force upon his recollection. Inspired by devotional feeling and a poetical genius of no mean order, he took up his pen, and the result was a metrical hymn in the Irish language, known as the "Feilire", or in Latin, as the *Festilogium* of St Ængus.[1] In this canticle, he enumerates some of the principal saints, whom he calls Princes of the Saints. The *Festilogium* is brief, although saints' festivals are assigned to each day of the week, with some allusions to characteristic virtues or actions of each holy individual therein commemorated. There is a commentary or series of notes found in the copies of this work, yet extant. These comments relate many particulars, regarding saints named in the *Festilogium*. We are at a loss to discover whether these notes are attributable to the saintly author of the poem itself, or to some scholiast belonging to a later age. The latter supposition, however, is more probable. It is recorded, that Ængus, about the year 804, presented a copy of this work to the learned lecturer, Fothadius, the Canonist, who returned this compliment by the bestowal of another work, of which he was author. This latter work is said to have been the famous Remonstrance he drew up, as addressed to King Aidus. It inveighs against the employment of ecclesiastics, in military services.[2]

---

[1] "A copy of his poem, called ' *Felire*', is preserved in the Leabhar Breac, in the Library of the Royal Irish Academy".—*Tracts Relating to Ireland, Muircheartach MacNeill's Circuit of Ireland*, page 32, *Mr. O'Donovan's Note* 36, *I.A.S.'s Publications.*

[2] The account regarding the expedition of Aedh Oirdnidhe is thus given at the year 799, [*recte* 804] in *O'Donovan's Annals of the Four Masters*, vol. i. pp. 408 to 411.   "Aedh Oirdnidhe assembled a very great army to proceed into Leinster, and devastated Leinster twice in one month.   A full muster of the men of Ireland (except the Leinster-men), both laity and clergy, was again made by him [and he marched] until he reached Dun-Cuair, on the confines of Meath and Leinster.   Thither came Connmhach, successor of Patrick, having the clergy of Leath-Chuinn along with him.   It was not pleasing to the clergy to go upon any expedition; they complained of their grievance to the king, and the king, i.e., Aedh, said that he would abide by the award of Fothadh na Canoine; on which occasion Fothadh passed the decision by which he exempted the clergy of Ireland for ever from expeditions and hostings, when he said:

    " The Church of the living God, let her alone, waste her not,
    Let her right be apart, as best it ever was.
    Every true monk, who is of a pure conscience ;
    For the Church to which it is due let him labour like every servant.
    Every soldier from that out, who is without [religious] rule or obedience,

The brevity, which characterises the Feilire, was a consequence of the object our saint appears to have had in view, whilst engaged in its composition. For, as he had resolved on imitating the practice of God's servant, whose remains were entombed at Coolbanagher, it would be inexpedient to introduce names of all the saints in his Festilogy. He was therefore obliged to confine himself to recording some of the principal ones. A recital of the entire Psalter, with his other daily exercises, left him no more than sufficient time, for the invocation and praises of saints included in his metrical hymn, which, it is said, formed a part of his diurnal devotions. According to a scholiast's account, left us in a preface to the Feilire, it would appear, that this poem had not been composed, in its completed form and in the same place. Some time must have elapsed from its first writing, to its final revision.[1] We are told, that the

> Is permitted to aid the great Aedh, son of Niall.
> This is the true rule, neither more nor less,
> Let every one serve in his vocation without murmur or complaint.
> The Church, etc.

" Aedh Oirdnidhe afterwards went to the King of Leinster, and obtained his full demand from the Leinster men; and Finsneachta, King of Leinster, gave him hostages and pledges". And at this passage, Mr. O'Donovan remarks, that the decision of Fothadh na Canoine, or Fothad " of the canon", is referred to in a preface to the *Felire-Aenguis*, preserved in the *Leabhar Breac*, fol. 32. On this occasion Fothadh wrote a poem by way of precept to the king, in which he advises him to exempt the clergy from the obligation of fighting his battles. There is a copy of the entire poem preserved in a vellum manuscript, in the Library of Trinity College, Dublin, H. 2. 18. It is also quoted in the *Leabhar-gabhala* of the O'Clerys, p. 199. *Ibid. n.* (e) pp. 409, 410. This decision of Fothadh obtained the name of a Canon; and after its issue, the clergy were exempted from attending military expeditions.

[1] The following is the account given of this poem by Mr. O'Reilly in his *Chronological account of nearly Four Hundred Irish Writers*, pp. liii. liv., when treating of Ængus. " He wrote a *Felire*, or Hierology, in Irish verse, giving an account of the festivals observed in the Church in his time. The *reimsceul*, or preliminary discourse, prefixed to this performance, gives the pedigree of the author, through several generations, by which it appears he was descended from Caelbach, King of Ulster, who defeated and killed Muiredhach Tireach, monarch of Ireland, at the battle of Port Righ, and succeeded him on the throne. The *Reimsceul* gives the time and place in which the author wrote this poem". After quoting a portion of this *reimsceul* in Irish, the following tranalation is given: " There are four co-necessaries in every learned treatise, i.e., place, time, person, and cause of writing. Therefore, the place of this piece was first Cúl Banagbar, in the plain of Rechet, in the country of *I Failge*, or O'Faly, and its revisal in Tamhlacht; (now Tallagh near Dublin) or else in Cluain Eidhnach it was begun, and in Cúl Banaghar it was finished, and revised in Tallaght. Ængus, moreover, was son of Oiblein, son of Fidrai, son of Dermod, son of Ainmirech, son of Cellair, son of Ænluaigh, son of Caelbaidh, son of Cruinba-draoi, son of Eochaidh Coba, son of Lughdhach, son of Fiacha Airidh, from whom are the Dal-Araidhe named. It is, moreover, the time of its writing the time of Conor, son of Aodh Oirdnighe, son of Niall *frasaigh*, for it was he who took the government of Ireland after Donagh, the son of Donall of Meath, King of Meath; for Angus, in the preface to the Felire, mentions the death of Donogh". The Felire is written in that kind of verse called by

poem had been commenced, either at Clonenagh or Cool-banagher, and that it had been revised at Tallaght. From the relation already given, we feel inclined rather to suppose, as the stay of Ængus at Coolbanagher appears to have been of no great duration, when about to pursue his way towards Tallaght, that his idea of writing the Feilire had been conceived only at the former place, and matured at the latter, where it would seem to have been solely written. It was most probably composed[1] after the year 797, the date for the death of Donogh, or Donnchadh, son to Donall.[2] Such conjecture agrees with

the Irish poets *rinn aird*, in which every verse ends with a word of two syllables, contains six syllables in the verse, and the entire *rann* twenty-four. It begins,

> "Re ꞃíl oáLac oáíneo
> Caíoeo ín ꞃí ꞃemaín
> íno ꞃo ꞃecc náꞃo naꞃáíL,
> Cꞃíꞃc hí CaLen enaíꞃ".

" Literal translation:

> " In the congregation of the seed of man,
> Went the king before us,
> Submitted to the noble law
> Christ, on the Calends of January".

* * * * * * *

" A copy of the *Felire*, beautifully written on vellum, is in the collection of the Assistant Secretary [O'Reilly.] From its orthography, and other internal marks of antiquity, it may be concluded that this MS. was written at least as early as the eleventh century, and is, perhaps, the oldest copy of that work now in existence. There is an entire copy in the *Leabhar Breac Mac Aedhagain*, or Speckled book of Mac Egan, in the Library of the Royal Irish Academy, and an imperfect copy on vellum in the same library".

1 During the progress of the late Ordnance Survey of Ireland the Felire or Festology of Ængus came first to be noticed, as a topographical tract of great value. Under the able superintendence of Sir Thomas Larcom and Dr. George Petrie, Eugene O'Curry brought it to bear, with important results, on our local topography, in every part of Ireland. The Rev. Dr. Todd suggested to the Board of Trinity College the engagement of Eugene O'Curry to make a *fac-simile* copy, for its library, of the *Leabhar Mor Dùna Doighré* or *Leabhar Breac*, in which the Festology is contained. On the Ordnance Survey Archaeological Department being dispensed with, Mr. George Smith, an eminent Dublin publisher, engaged Mr. O'Curry to transcribe the Festology, once more, with a view to its publication. " This, however, was not a *fac-simile* copy, which indeed it would be practically useless to print, even if such a thing were possible, because the tract consists, properly, of three parts; namely, the text of the poem, the interlined gloss, and the interlined marginal, topographical, and other notes". These three parts were distinctly copied, all the contractions were lengthened out, and the whole disposed and arranged in such a manner as to merit the approval of our most distinguished Irish scholars. This copy was afterwards collated with other MS. in London and Oxford. Yet, the copy thus prepared has not been published; the transcript and translation into English remained in the possession of Mr. Smith, who, we believe, has since transferred this copy to the Royal Irish Academicians.

2 O'Donovan's *Annals of the Four Masters*, vol. i. n. (r.), p. 399, where we read : " O'Flaherty places the accession of Donnchadh in the year 770, and his death in 797, which is the true chronology. He adds: " Quo rege, Anno 795, Dani Scotiæ, et Hiberniæ oras infestare coparunt".—*Ogygia*, p. 433". The

that of Colgan, that the *scholia* on the Festilogy of Ængus had been composed at Tallagh in the time of Malruan.[1]

V.—*Description and analysis of St. Ængus' Festology.—He resided at Dysart Bethach at the period of its completion.—Its first circulation in the reign of Aidus the Sixth.—The Martyrology of Tallagh, and interesting particulars regarding this composition.*

We are indebted to the late distinguished Irish scholar, Professor Eugene O'Curry, for a particular description and analysis of Ængus' metrical Festology or *Féliré*.[2] This composition consists of three distinct parts. The *first part*, known as the Invocation, contains five quatrains, which ask grace and sanctification from Christ on the poet's work. It is written in the ancient *Conachlann*, or what modern Gaelic scholars call "chain-verse", in English. By such metrical arrangement, the last words of each quatrain are identical, or nearly so, with the first words of that succeeding.[3] The *second part*, as we are told, is

Annals of Ulster, however, assign the death of this monarch to A.D. 798, and the *Four Masters* to A.D. 792. I am unable to discover any notice regarding Conor, Son of Aodh Oirdnighe, mentioned by the scholiast on Ængus' poem, in any of our early Annals.

[1] Of this *Féliré* or Festology—sometimes called the Martyrology of Aengus Ceilé Dé—six copies, at least, are known to be extant, and four of these are on vellum. Two copies are preserved in the Bodleian Library, Oxford ; one, if not two, at St. Isidore's College, Rome ; one in the Burgundian Library, Brussels ; one, a transcript, made for Dr. Todd, by Professor O'Curry ; and one, found in the celebrated *Leabhar Mór Dúna Doighré*—commonly called the *Leabhar Breac*—compiled about the year 1400, and now in possession of the Royal Irish Academy, Dublin. "There is a short history of the author, and the tract prefixed to this copy, which commenced, as such Gaedhlic documents usually do, with giving the name of the author, the time, the place, and the object of the composition. There is, then, a short disquisition on this arrangement, in which the usages of the philosophers and the order of the creation are referred to as precedents". See *Lectures on the Manuscript Materials of Ancient Irish History*, Lect. xvii. p. 363.

[2] In O'Reilly's *Chronological Account of nearly Four Hundred Irish Writers*, p. liii., it receives the designation of a Hierology.

[3] An illustration, in the Irish language and character, will be found in *Lectures on the Manuscript Materials of Ancient Irish History*, Appendix No. cxiii. p. 610, and which has been published from the original, contained in the *Leabhar Breac*—a MS. belonging to the Royal Irish Academy. The five stanzas in Irish have been thus rendered into English, by Mr. O'Curry:—

> "Sanctify, O Christ! my words :—
> O Lord of the seven heavens!
> Grant me the gift of wisdom,
> O Sovereign of the bright sun!
>
> O bright sun, who dost illumine
> The heavens with all thy holiness!
> O King who governest the angels !
> O Lord of all the people!

2

a poem, by way of preface, and it consists of two hundred and twenty quatrains. But of these only eighty are found prefixed to the main poem, or chief subject matter. The remaining one hundred and forty quatrains are postfixed to the main poem, and these are called the post or second preface, by Mr. O'Curry. We may rather, perhaps, consider them in the light of those verses, which many of our medieval and modern poets designate the "L'Envoy", as the conclusion of a poem. The verses are in a similar character, and follow the like measure, as they are indeed a continuation of the Invocation. The eighty stanzas prefixed to the main poem, in very beautiful and forcible language give us a very glowing account regarding the sufferings and tortures of the early Christian martyrs; how their persecutors' names have been forgotten, while those of their victims were remembered with honour, veneration, and affection; how Pilate's wife sinks into oblivion, while the Blessed Virgin Mary has been remembered and venerated from earth's uttermost bounds to its centre. Even in Ireland, the enduring supremacy of Christ's Church had been manifested. Tara had been abandoned and become a desert, because its kings were vain-glorious, while Armagh remains the populous seat of dignity, piety, and learning. Cruachain, a former royal residence of the Connaught kings, is deserted, while Clonmacnois resounds with the dashing of chariots and tramp of multitudes to honour St. Ciaran's shrine. Aillinn's royal palace had passed away, while St. Brigid's church at Kildare retained its dazzling splendour. Ul-

> O Lord of the people!
> O King all righteous and good!
> May I receive the full benefit
> Of praising Thy royal hosts.
>
> Thy royal hosts I praise,
> Because Thou art my Sovereign;
> I have disposed my mind
> To be constantly beseeching Thee.
>
> I beseech a favour from Thee,
> That I be purified from my sins
> Through the peaceful bright-shining flock,
> The royal host whom I celebrate".

We are informed, that General Vallancey and Theophilus O'Flanagan, having met with this poem—which is rather a conspicuous one—in the *Leabhar Breac*, and finding the name of Christ contractedly written CR, with a horizontal dash over these two letters, considered they had found an address to the sun. This was a supposed proof of the former worship of that luminary by the ancient Irish. The letters C R were presumed to have been a contraction for *Creas*, which, from the books of Indian Brahmins and the Sanscrit, Vallancey conjectured to be a name for the sun, common both to Ireland and India. These views of General Vallancey, with a highly poetical translation of Aengus' poem, were embodied in a small printed pamphlet. This was addressed "To the President and Members of the Royal Irish Academy, as a proof of the Ancient History of Ireland", by General Vallancey.

ster's royal palace at Emania had disappeared, while the holy Coemghen's church at Glcann-da-locha remains in full glory. The monarch Leaghaire's pomp and pride were extinguished, while St. Patrick's name continues to shine with undiminished lustre. Thus, the poet continues to contrast fleeting and forgotten names and reputations of great men and establishments, belonging to the pagan and secular world, with the stability, freshness, and splendour of Christian Churches, and the everflourishing names of their illustrious, although often humble founders. The *third part* is properly the *Félire* or Festological Poem itself, and it is comprised within three hundred and sixtyfive quatrains, which, the reader will observe, forms a stanza for each day in the year. The Circumcision of our Lord is placed at the head of the Festivals, and with it the *Félire* begins.[1] This poem is not wholly confined to notices of the Irish saints. Our great national Apostle, St. Patrick, is commemorated at the 17th of March.[2] And again, at the 13th of April, Bishop Tassagh, one of St. Patrick's favourite companions, is recorded.[3] Bishop Tassagh was chief manufacturer and ornamenter of croziers, crosses, bells, and shrines, and attended St. Patrick at his death.

The whole of this, which is the chief poem, as also the first preface, is thickly interlined with an ancient gloss and commentary. These explain difficult or obsolete words and passages. Sometimes, notes may be found on the sites of ancient churches, connected with our Irish saints, who lived to the time of our author. Occasional passages from their Lives and Miracles will be seen. These notes are interspersed over the margin, and

---

[1] In the *Lectures on the Manuscript Materials of Ancient Irish History*, Appendix No. cxiv. p. 611, may be seen the first stanza of this part of the poem in the Irish language and character, as extracted from the original found in the *Leabhar Breac*, R. I. A. It has been thus rendered into English by Mr. O'Curry:—

" At the head of the congregated saints,
     Let the King take the first place :
     Unto the noble dispensation did submit
     Christ—on the calends of January".

[2] See *Ibid.*, *Appendix*, No. cxv. for the Irish stanza thus rendered into English:—

" The blaze of a splendid sun,
     The apostle of stainless Erinn,
     Patrick—with his countless thousands,
     May he shelter our wretchedness".

[3] See *Ibid.*, *Appendix*, No. cxvi., for the Irish stanza, thus rendered into English :—

" The kingly Bishop Tassagh,
     Who administered on his arrival,
     The body of Christ—the truly powerful King —
     And the Communion to Patrick".

they require close and accurate study to connect them with their appropriate textual passages. The three parts, or cantos, into which the entire poem has been divided, may be treated, indeed, as one continuous composition. The last words of the Invocation are the first words to the first preface of eighty stanzas; while the last words of this preface are the first words of the main poem; and again, the last words of this chief poem are the first words of the post or second preface, which consists of one hundred and forty stanzas.

This latter division concludes the work, and in it Ængus recapitulates the subject of his *Féliré*, teaching the faithful how to read and use it, and explaining its arrangement. He declares, though great the number, he has only been able to enumerate the princes of the saints in it. He recommends it for pious meditation to the faithful, and indicates spiritual benefits to be gained by reading or reciting it. He says, he had travelled far and near to collect the names and history of subjects for his praise and invocation. For the foreign saints, he consulted St. Ambrose, St. Jerome, and Eusebius. He collected the festivals of our Irish saints from " the countless hosts of the illuminated books of Erinn". He then says, having already mentioned and invoked the saints at their respective festival days, he will now invoke them in classes or bands, under certain heads or leaders. This is done in the following order: The elders or ancients, under Noah; the prophets under Isaiah; the patriarchs under Abraham; the apostles and disciples under Peter; the wise or learned men under Paul; the martyrs under Stephen; the spiritual directors under old Paul; the Virgins of the World under the Blessed Virgin Mary; the holy bishops of Rome under Peter; the bishops of Jerusalem under Jacob or James; the bishops of Antioch also under Peter; the bishops of Alexandria under Mark; a division of them under Honorati; a division of learned men under the gifted Benedict; all the innocents who suffered at Bethlehem under Georgius; the priests under Aaron; the monks under Anthony; a division of the world's saints under Martin; the noble saints of Erinn under St. Patrick; the saints of Scotland under St. Colum Cille; while the last great division of Erinn's saintly virgins has been placed under holy St. Brigid of Kildare. In an eloquent strain, Aengus then continues to beseech our Saviour's mercy for himself and for all mankind, through the merits and sufferings of those saints he has named and enumerated. He asks through the merits of their dismembered bodies; through their bodies pierced with lances; through

---

[1] The Felire or Festologies are closely connected with lives of the saints. That of Aengus especially receives the praise of M. de la Villemarque in the November number of the French periodical, *Le Correspondant*, for 1863.

their wounds; through their groans; through their relics; through
their blanched countenances; through their bitter tears; through
all the sacrifices offered of the Saviour's own Body and Blood,
as it is in Heaven, upon the holy altars; through the blood that
flowed from the Saviour's own side; through his sacred Humanity;
and through His Divinity in union with the Holy Spirit and the
Heavenly Father. After this long invocation, Aengus says the
brethren of his order deemed all his prayers and petitions too
little; whereupon, he resolves to change his course, that no one
may have cause for complaint. Then, he commences another
moving appeal to our Lord for himself and all men. He beseeches mercy according to the merciful worldly interposition of
Divine clemency in times past. Thus Enoch and Elias had
been saved from dangers in this world; Noah had been saved
from the deluge; Abraham had been saved from plagues and
from the Chaldeans; Lot had been saved from the burning city;
Jonas had escaped from the whale; Isaac had been delivered
from his father's hands. He entreats Jesus, through intercession of his Holy Mother, to save him, as Jacob was saved
from the hands of his brother, and as John [Paul] was saved
from the viper's venom. He again recurs to examples found
in the Old Testament He mentions the saving of David
from Goliath's sword; the saving of Susanna from her dangers;
of Nineveh from destruction; of the Israelites from Mount
Gilba [Gilboa]; of Daniel from the lions' den; of Moses from
the hands of Faro [Pharaoh]; of the three youths from the
fiery furnace; of Tobias from his blindness; of Peter and Paul
from the dungeon; of Job from demoniac tribulations; of David
from Saul; of Joseph from his brothers' hands; of the Israelites
from Egyptian bondage; of Peter from the sea-waves; of John
from the fiery caldron; of Martin from the priest of the idol.
Again, he beseeches Jesus, through intercession of the Heavenly
household, to be saved, as St. Patrick had been, from the
poisoned drink at Teamhar [Tara], and as St Coemhghin
[Kevin] had been at Gleann dâ locha [Glendalough], from perils
of the mountain.[1]

St. Aengus, we are told, resided at his church, in a place called
Disert Bethech,[2] which lay on the northern bank of the river
n-Eoir—now the Nore—and a few miles above the present Mon-
asterevan, in the Queen's County. This, however, must be an in-
correct topographical description of the locality. Aengus had
then just finished his Festology. A friendship was here
formed between our saint and Fothadh the canonist, who showed
the poem he had composed for Aedh's decision. Before pre-

---

[1] See *Manuscript Materials of Ancient Irish History.* Lect. xvii. pp. 365 to 370.
[2] We feel inclined to believe this place was not distinct from Dysart Enos.

senting it to the king, he desired and received the warm approval of his brother poet.[1]

It is said, Aengus Ceilé De first published or circulated his "Festology" that year when Aideus the Sixth, surnamed Oirdnidhe, undertook his expedition against the Leinster people, A.D. 804, according to the most correct supposition. At this time, Aedh encamped at Disert Bethech. Fothadius, the Canonist, accompanied him. This learned man is said to have received a present of the *Feilire*, which had been first shown to him, from our saint's hands. Fothadh solemnly approved and recommended it for perusal by the faithful.[2] Thus, it would appear, that the poem had not been issued, until after the death of holy Abbot Malruan, which took place A.D. 792, according to the best computation.[3] This fact appears still more evident, as in the Festilogy, the name of Tallagh's venerable superior is found recorded, with a suitable eulogy. Professor O'Curry says, that according to the best accounts, Aengus wrote his poem in or before A.D. 798; for, so far as can be ascertained, the name of any saint, who died after such date, cannot be discovered in it.[4]

According to Colgan, Aengus had resolved upon commencing another work, in which should be included the names of saints, omitted in his Feilire, that thus any doubt regarding the veneration due to them, and the intentional omission of their names in his poem, might in a measure be obviated.

In conjunction with St. Molruan, it is said, he undertook the compilation of another work, named usually *Martyrologium Aengussii filii Hua-Oblenii et Moelruanii*, "the Martyrology of Aengus and Molruan". It is sometimes known as *Martyrologium Tamlactense*, "the Martyrology of Tallaght". This work, which some consider prior to the *Festilogium*, in the order of being composed, is prosaic and very comprehensive.[5] For every day,

[1] See *Ibid.*, p. 364.

[2] See *Ibid.*, p. 364; also Colgan's *Acta Sanctorum Hiberniae, xi. Martii. Vita S. Aengussii*, cap. xiii. p. 581.

[3] Such is the correction of Mr. O'Donovan, although the *Four Masters* place his death at A.D. 787. See O'Donovan's *Annals of the Four Masters*, vol. i. pp. 392, 393.

[4] See *Lectures on the Manuscript Materials of Ancient Irish History*. Lect. xvii. p. 362.

[5] In the summer of 1849, Mr. Eugene O'Curry and Dr. Todd examined the MS. collections in the University of Oxford, for four days spent there; and during their stay, so far as time permitted, they extracted various readings, considered desirable and useful, from the Festilogium of Aengus. These were intended to further illustrate Mr. O'Curry's transcript of this poem. Amongst other valuable documents, they discovered two fine copies of the Martyrology of Aengus the Culdee, and the *Psalter-na-Rann*, comprising five books on the Irish Saints, by the same author. During this year, also, Mr. O'Curry spent some months in the British Museum, London, having his transcribed copy of the Festilogy with him. It appears now, that this work was inaccurately noticed by Edward O'Reilly in his "Irish Writers", at the year 800; by Dr. O'Connor,

a list of foreign saints was first set down, and then followed the
names of our Irish saints. Colgan considers this work the most
copious of all the martyrologies he had ever seen.[1] Yet, it would
seem to have been extremely defective, in parts. The names
of many saints, omitted in the Roman and other martyrologies,
are to be found in the first part of the Martyrology attributed
to Æengus and Molruan. However, a learned authority supposes,
that Æengus composed a still more ancient Martyrology, which
deserves to bear his name, and that this is the oldest Irish Martyr-

[j]n his " Stowe Catalogue", page 30, note 3 ; and in Harris's Ware " Irish
Writers", page 53. The Irish Archæological Society has announced the intention of supplying a *desideratum* long felt in native literature, by publishing at
a future period " The Hagiographical Works of St. Æengus the Culdee". We
fear, however, an indefinite postponement.

[1] This opinion he must have entertained, however, before the OClerys had
prepared the celebrated one, now popularly known as " The Martyrology of
Donegall". See *Acta Sanctorum Hiberniæ, xi. Martii. Vita S. Æengussii*, cap.
xii. p. 581. At note 10, affixed to this passage we find the following interesting
statement. Father Heribert Roswede, a man deeply versed in ecclesiastical
antiquities, had received from the Carthusians at Treves, or Triers, in Germany,
a certain very ancient codex, belonging to St. Willebrord's Monastery at Epternac, in Triers diocese, and in the duchy of Luxemburg. It contained an ex-
ceedingly old and most complete Martyrology. This included names of many
saints for each day, not found in the *Martyrologium Romanum*, or in any other
Martyrology hitherto edited. He thought this was the Martyrology of St
Jerome, and that it should have been thus designated, owing to the prefixed
title : *Christe fave votis. Codex S. Willebrordi continet Martyrologium Hieronymi.*
Whether this had been the Martyrology ascribed to St. Jerome, or to St
Eusebius, or to St. Willebrord, in most particulars, Colgan says, it agreed with
the Martyrology of St. Æengus, or with the Martyrology of Tallagh. Only, in
this latter, those places where the Martyrs suffered were more accurately noted,
and it had the advantage of being more copious. The Martyrology of Tallagh has also added at each day certain Irish saints, and frequently some other
saints, wanting in the Epternac copy. Two reasons incline Colgan to believe
that St. Willebrord brought that Martyrology—which is known as *Codex S.
Wilebrordi* or *Epternacensi*—with him, when he left Ireland on his way to Epternac. *First,* two copies had been preserved in Colgan's time, although differing somewhat in certain places. These belonged to Ireland. One of them had
been transmitted to Louvain. It was written on old vellum, but it was not
found in a perfect state. Each day, the other copy had been expected " ex quo
Sanctos Hiberniæ jam excerptos accepimus". No other copy of this work was
known to be extant in any of the European libraries, that only excepted which
belonged to the collection of Epernac MSS. *Secondly,* one of these copies
seems to have its authenticity proved correlatively with the other. For St.
Willebrord, whose Codex has his name inscribed, and whose very handwriting
can be traced in part, with every appearance of certain proof, did not come
from Anglia—as some writers say—but he came from Hibernia immediately
to Friesland or Frisia, and thence to Epternac. Willebrord had previously
lived in Ireland, from the twentieth to the thirty-third year of his age, engaged
in scholastic studies and in practices of piety, as Alovinus Flaccus states in his
Life, and as Venerable Bede has it in his *Historia Ecclesiastica Gentis Anglo-
rum,* Lib. v. cap. 10, 11, and 12. For the truth of these statements, Colgan
cites other authorities, in the Life of St. Suithbert, at the first day of March.
It is not at all probable, that Willebrord found the aforesaid Martyrology in
the territory of Frisia, or in other adjoining districts, in a great measure in-
habited only by unbelievers. Nor has any similar copy been there discovered.
On the contrary, Colgan asserts that many such copies were to be found in
Ireland when he wrote. As here mentioned, in the Life of St. Æengus, the

ology known.[1] As Ængus, in his metrical work, "The Festilogium", cites the martyrologies attributed to Jerome and Eusebius, it is highly probable, that he must have used these works, now supposed to be lost, while engaged at the compilation of his own writings.[2] Nay more, might it not be possible, that the first part of this Martyrology is, to some extent, a transcript from that ascribed to Eusebius or to Jerome? And what delight and interest would not the lovers of ecclesiastical history take in the discovery of such identity, could it only be proved! If a conjecture of this kind should be well founded, the writings so much regretted by the learned as lost, because not hitherto discovered, might in part—if not altogether—be found among unpublished MSS. of an Irish saint, yet mouldering on the shelves of some Irish or continental library. In the latter supposition, probably it may be established that such Martyrology had been carried from our island to its present place of preservation.

We feel inclined to believe, that the Martyrology of Tallagh had been written—but perhaps not in its completed state—before Ængus had composed his *Féliré*. Nor does it follow, because Blathmac, who had been martyred for the faith at Iona on the 19th July, A.D. 823, and Feidhlimidh Mac Crimhthainn,

Martyrologies, ascribed both to Eusebius and to St. Jerome, were extant in his time, or before A.D. 787, when such testimony is supposed to have been recorded. These martyrologies are considered to be oldest compilations of the kind. See *Ibid.*, p. 582.

[1] See Professor Eugene O'Curry's *Lectures on the Manuscript Materials of Ancient Irish History*, Lect. xvii. pp. 362, 363, 364. Yet, in Father Michael O'Clery's preface to a poem of Marianus Gorman, he states, that the Martyrology of Ængus Ceilé De had been composed from the Martyrology of Tamlacht. In this latter, the names and dates for two holy men are found, and both died many years after Ængus himself. "These are *Blathmac*, the son of Flann, monarch of Erinn, who died for the faith, at the hands af the Danes, in the island of Hi, or Iona, on the 19th of July, in the year 823; and *Feidhlimidh Mac Crimhthainn*, King of Munster, who died on the 18th of August, in the year 845, according to the *Annals of the Four Masters*, but whose festival is placed in the kalendar at the 28th of August". It is supposed, according to the best accounts, that Ængus wrote his work in or before A.D. 798, and so far as Mr. O'Curry ascertained, "no saint is found in it who died after that year". Wherefore, it would appear, that St. Ængus composed a Martyrology, distinct from that known as the Tallagh Martyrology. However, it seems to be the case, this Martyrology of St. Ængus must have been identical with his Festilogy.

[2] It must be remarked that D'Achery, in his *Spicilegium, sive Collectio Veterum aliquot Scriptorum*, has published " Martyrologium vetustissimum Sancti Hieronymi Presbyteri nomine insignitum". *Tomus Quartus.* This is even imperfect, since he appends the following remarks:—" Cætera legi non potuerunt in MS. utpote a tineis corrosa; silicet ab hac die ad viii. Kal. Jan. a quo incipit hocce Martyrologium". It must be confessed, if this Martyrology, for the most part, were written by St. Jerome, it has been interpolated by some one, who lived since his time, as the names of many among the more recent saints are contained in it. See the remarks of Henry Valeisius, in his Appendix to the edition of *Eusebius's Ecclesiastical History*, on this subject. The edition of the Martyrology of Tallaght, published by the Rev. Dr. Kelly, must have been prepared from a copy, differing from that more complete one, described by Colgan; since it only contains the names of Irish, and omits the list of foreign saints.

King of Munster, who died on the 18th of August, A.D. 845, have been entered in it, that these names had not been introduced in copies, transcribed after the death of Ængus.[1] As we are not likely ever to recover the original copy of the Tallagh Martyrology, criticism must remain at fault, in reference to its real author or authors.

We find a more accurate description of what has been called the Hieronyman Tallagh Martyrology, than had been furnished either by Colgan or Bollandus.[2] This comes from the pen of Father John Baptist Soller.[3] It does not appear that Bollandus had ever seen Colgan's copy; but Soller, however, inspected and describes it as containing ten vellum *folia* of large size, with nearly half a leaf, and covered with another leaf of similar material and appearance. In the commencement of this Codex, some modern hand has inscribed it, *Martyrologium Tamlactense, et Opuscula S. Aengussi Keledei.* In two different places it is noted, as having belonged to the convent of Donegall. Those leaves were not clearly traced nor well arranged. Many names in this Codex were almost illegible. It was defective from iv of the Kalends of February to the iv of the Ides of March; so that the months of January and March were not perfect. The whole of February was missing. The April month was alone complete. May ran on to the 20th day, or to the xiii of the Kalends of June. June and July were wanting. August began from the iv Nones, but its remaining days were preserved. In September were missing the xii, xi, and x days of the October Kalends. October continued to the iii of the Kalends of November. The whole of November was missing. December commenced only at xv of the Kalends of January. Soller declares, after a diligent examination, he could easily observe that this Codex had been over-rated by the members of his society. Papebroke had frequently mentioned to him that Colgan or the Irish Minorite Fathers at Louvain had merely sent extracts of this copy to Bollandus. Besides the insertion of Irish proper names in this Martyrology, there were found other festivals, added by a comparatively modern hand. Among these, he notices the feast of St. Joseph, the Revelation of St. Michael the Archangel, the festival of All Saints, and many other solemni-

---

[1] Mr. O'Curry, from circumstances already alluded to, seems to doubt if Aengus had anything to do with its authorship. See *Lectures on the Manuscript Materials of Ancient Irish History*, Lect. xvii. p. 362.

[2] Bollandus has published some extracts from Colgan's copy, " *sub nomine* Martyrologia Hieronymiani *Tamlactensis*", at the last days of the January month in his *Acta Sanctorum.*

[3] See *Acta Sanctorum, tomus* vi., in his learned Preface to a new edition of Usuard's Martyrology. In this he treats regarding various copies of the Martyrology ascribed to St. Jerome, cap. 1, art. 1, §§ 1, 2.

3

ties of a like description. After this Martyrology, Soller found a list of what he conjectures to be Irish names, running through three leaves. In fine, there were *opuscula* or fragments of tracts in the Irish language, of which he was entirely ignorant. This Soller declares to be a complete description of the Codex.[1]

Of the Martyrology, attributed to Ængus and Molruan, Colgan appears to have possessed two copies. Even these were not entire. The names of saints are simply set down in this work, which, for stated reasons, he preferred calling the Martyrology of Tallagh or Tamlacht. In the *first place*, it had been composed by joint labour on the part of Ængus and Molruan, at Tallagh. *Secondly*, because it could not be cited as the work of both saints, without tediousness and confusion; the more so, as he had been obliged frequently to quote another Martyrology, the sole production of Ængus. *Thirdly*, because it is reasonably conjectured, that ancient writers called it the Martyrology of Tamlacht. Thus, Marianus Gorman, who lived more than five hundred years before Colgan's time, in the preface to his Martyrology remarks, that St. Ængus composed his metrical Festilogy, from the Martyrology of Tamlacht, which had previously been written. The latter work, therefore, was supposed to differ in no respect from the Martyrology of Ængus and Melruan, which had been composed at Tallaght. There was no other Martyrology known to be extant in Colgan's time, and that could better deserve the title of the Tallagh Martyrology, or which, in fact, was distinguished by this latter appellation. *Fourthly*, the work entitled, "Martyrology of Ængus and Mœlruan", contains the names of its reputed authors and other saints, who were their contemporaries, but who departed this life after their time. Among others, we find recorded therein the name, St. Corpre, Bishop of Clonmacnoise, who died A.D. 899; but we do not find the name of St. Cormac Mac Cuileannan, king and bishop, who departed this life in the earlier part of the tenth century, nor, in fact, of any saint, who died after A.D. 900. Hence, Colgan is under an impression, that certain subsequent additions were made to the joint work of Ængus and Melruan, by some monk belonging to the monastery of Tallagh, who lived towards the close of the ninth, and who died in the beginning of the tenth century[2]

An opinion was entertained by some ancient writers, that this Martyrology and the Feilire had been composed by Ængus at Tallaght, whilst engaged in following the humbler

---

[1] See *ibid.*, § 2, . vii.
[2] Colgan's *Acta Sanctorum Hiberniae*, xi. *Martii. Vita S. Ængussii*, cap. xii. p. 581. In Harris' *Ware*, a similar opinion has been adopted. See vol. iii. *Writers of Ireland*, book i. chap. v. p. 52.

duties of a farm servant. Sufficient evidence can be adduced, however, to prove, that the *Feilire* could not have been issued until some years after St. Melruan's death. The title prefixed to the Martyrology is couched in those terms: " Incipit Martyrologium Ængussii, filii Hua-oblenii et Melruanii". It shows, that both saints must have been joint labourers at the work, previous to the death of Melruan, in the year 792, although some additions were undoubtedly made in the succeeding century. Wherefore, Marianus Gorman, in the preface to his Martyrology, has rightly observed, in Colgan's opinion, that St. Ængus took the saints, named in his Festilogy, from the Martyrology of Tallagh, which had been first composed.[1]

---

[1] See Colgan's *Acta Sanctorum Hiberniae, xi. Martii. Vita S. Ængussii,* cap. xiii. p. 581. Dr. Ledwich strives to show, that this Martyrology was first written in the ninth century, because it has the names of Moelruan, Aengus, and other later saints. See *Antiquities of Ireland,* p. 365. " It is true that, considered in its present state", says Dr. Lanigan, " it was not completed until even the end of that century; but does it follow that Aengus and Moelruan had no share in drawing it up? He adds, that in its second preface, it cites the Martyrology of St. Jerome. Here the doctor is wrong; for this martyrology is quoted, not in any preface to the Martyrology of Tallagh, *alias* that of Aengus and Moelruan, but in the second preface to the *Festilogium* of Aengus (See *AA. SS.* p. 581). He then tells us that the Martyrology called *of St. Jerome,* was not known until about the ninth century; but might not *about the ninth century,* be implied to take in part of the eighth, prior to Aengus having been engaged in any of these works? The Doctor says that Launoy has proved, that this martyrology was fabricated about the ninth century. Now in the passage, which he refers to, Launoy has not even attempted to prove it; and all that he says, is that the martyrology called *of St. Jerome* cannot be proved to have been written by that saint on any authority prior to the reign of Charlemagne. But the Doctor cares nothing about inaccuracies and misquotations, provided he could make the reader believe, that martyrologies are not to be depended upon. Yet Launoy was, in the little he has said, mistaken; for the martyrology ascribed to St. Jerome, or rather to Eusebius and St. Jerome, as quoted by Aengus, is mentioned more than once by Bede, who lived many years before Charlemagne. Thus he cites (*L.* 2 *in Marcum,* cap. 26) *Martyrologium Eusebii et Hieronymi vocabulis insignitum;* and (*Retract. in Act. Ap.* cap. i.) he states, that Eusebius is said to have been the author, and Jerome the translator (See more in Bollandus' General Preface, cap. 4. § 4. at 1 January). That Eusebius compiled a sort of Martyrology is considered certain (*ib.,* cap. i. § 3); and the learned Bollandists, Henschenius and Papebrochius (*Prolog. ad Martyrol. Bed.* at *March,* Tom. 2) were inclined to think, that it was not only translated, but likewise augmented by St. Jerome. Be this as it may, it is well known, that what is now called the *Martyrology of St. Jerome* was not written by him; but, it is supposed to have been originally compiled, not long after his time, and is considered by many very learned men to be the oldest extant. D'Achery has published it (*Spicileg.* Tom. 4), and in his *Monitum* states from Henry Valois, that it was used by Gregory the Great, and existed many years earlier. Since those times some names have been added to it, such as that of Gregory himself, which D'Achery has marked in Italics. Among these is that of St. Patrick, and perhaps the Doctor had heard so, on which account he wished to deny its antiquity. Much more might be said on this subject, were this the place for doing so. Meanwhile the reader may consult also Tillemont, *Hist. Eccl.* tom. xii. at *St. Jerome,* art. 144". See Dr. Lanigan's *Ecclesiastical History of Ireland,* vol. iii. chap. xx. § x. n. 102, pp. 249, 250,

Mr. O'Curry appears to attribute this preface to the pen of Father Michael O'Clery. The Martyrology of Tallagh is generally believed to be the oldest Martyrology of our Irish saints known to be extant; and with their festival days it often records the immediate fathers and churches of our national saints. The Martyrology of Tallagh has been published by the late Rev. Professor Matthew Kelly, D.D., of Maynooth College. In the year 1847, he procured a copy, partially defective, from the Burgundian Library at Brussels, and this he published in 1857, just before his lamented death. Its defects have been supplied, in parts, from other Irish Martyrologies. It contains valuable historic notes and additions.[1] However, it is to be regretted, that the learned editor had not been able to obtain a more complete—yet still deficient—copy for publication, which Colgan had once procured. Indeed, a number of similar copies, had they been available, must have greatly enhanced the value and accuracy of such an interesting work.

VI.—*St. Ængus was probably ordained Priest at Tallaght.— Treatise of St. Ængus " De Sanctis Hiberniae".—The " Sal- tair-na-rann".—Pedigrees of Irish Saints attributed to his authorship.*

Although Aengus is said to have become a professed monk in Clonenagh Monastery, and to have concealed the fact of his enrolment in the ecclesiastical order, when he sought admission to Maelruan's Monastery at Tallagh,[2] it is probable, our saint had only received clerical tonsure, or at most minor orders, when he first left Dysartenos. Were Aengus advanced to the priesthood at this period of life, a necessity for celebrating the holy sacrifice of Mass very frequently,[3] with the performance of other peculiar sacerdotal functions, must soon have revealed his rank to Abbot Maelruan, and to the members of his community. Even were those solitary or strictly private Masses, formerly permitted to be

[1] In 1849, the Rev. Dr. Todd likewise procured from the Belgian government the loan of a MS. containing this, as well as O'Gorman's and Aengus' Martyrologies, all in Father Michael O'Clery's handwriting. Professor O'Curry made accurate transcripts from it, for Dr. Todd's private library. See *Lectures on the Manuscript Materials of Ancient Irish History*, Lect. xvii. pp. 362, 363.

[2] Regarding the first statement, Colgan says of him, " Monachum professus in nobili monasterio de Cluain-edhneach", and in the second instance, " clericale institutum occultans". See *Acta Sanctòrum Hiberniae, xi. Martii. Vita S. Aengussii*, cap. ii. v., pp. 579, 580.

[3] See that very learned treatise of Cardinal Bona, *Rerum Liturgicarum de his quae ad Missam generatim spectant*, Lib. i. cap. iv. pp. 203, 204, for proofs of frequently offering the Holy Victim of propitiation, and from the earliest ages of the Christian Church. *Opera Omnia Emin. Dom. D. Joannis Bona, S. R. E. Card. Pres. Ord. Cis.* Antwerp edition, A.D. 1723, folio.

celebrated in many ancient churches,[1] allowed as a practice in our early religious houses, the secret of our saint's priestly ordination could not long be concealed. It is more difficult to comprehend how, as a monk, he had not been questioned on the subject of his having already received the peculiar and noticeable ecclesiastical tonsure. However, there can hardly be any doubt, after Abbot Maelruan discovered the real name, virtues, and learning of his highly-gifted disciple, with his dispositions for the office, Aengus must soon have been raised to the sacerdotal dignity. For want of more complete records, referring to our saint's biography, not having seen many early copies of his works, and with little serving for autobiography in his own writings, our present imperfect lights, regarding his private acts, occasionally require us to launch upon a sea of conjecture.

Towards the saints of his country, Ængus seems to have entertained an extraordinary veneration. According to Colgan's account, he wrote five distinct books, "De Sanctis Hiberniae", which treat, in a particular manner, about their several lives, or on matters pertaining to them. In the first book, he gives the different distinctions of these saints in classes; he enumerates three hundred and forty-five bishops, two hundred and ninety-nine abbots and priests, and seventy-eight deacons. These he has comprised within the limits of three chapters. The second book is known as the "Homonymi", or the enumeration of saints bearing similar names, but distinguished by various other titles. It mentions eight hundred and fifty-five distinct persons, under sixty-two different names, and it is divided into two parts; the first part containing fifty chapters, on holy men of the same name, and the second twelve chapters on holy women. The third book, known as the "Book of Sons", divides the saints into another classification. It names saints who are descended from the same father, and afterwards only sons, each cited by the father's name. Lastly, are enumerated female saints, in their descent from the same father. The names of ninety-four fathers,[2] who had one saint, or more saints than one as children, are here preserved, although the number of saints cannot be

---

[1] Cardinal Bona, *Rerum Liturgicarum de his quae ad Missam generatim spectant.* Having described different rites for celebrating the Holy Sacrifice, he remarks: "actas aliquando in Monasteriis Missas a solo sacerdote nemine praesente et respondente, quae idcirco solitariae dictae sint" . . . Verum Missas privatas non a Monachis, sed a primae Ecclesiae Patribus originem traxisse capite sequenti ostendam: Missas autem solitarias in coenobiis actas ex indulgentia, ut loquitur Eduensis, sive ex privilegio; canonicae sanctiones demonstrant, quae sublatis omnibus privilegiis, ne quis solus Missas ageret, districte prohibuerunt". Lib. i. cap. xiii. p. 230.

[2] Colgan adds, "omissis aliquot aliis, quae prae nimia exesi codicis vetustate legi non possunt". *Acta Sanctorum Hiberniae, xi. Martii. Vita S. Ængussii,* cap. xiv. p. 581.

discovered. The fourth book comprises the names of two hundred and ten saints, with their maternal genealogy. It would appear from this title, that the paternal genealogy of those saints had been previously written, either by another hand, or by that of Ængus. The fifth "Book of Litanies" enumerates, in form of an invocation, a long list of saints. In several of its invocations, the principal name, with associated disciples, is generally found. This name usually pertains to the saint who presided over a particular monastery, with the number of holy disciples under his rule; or a saint who was buried at some particular church, with his companions, who "slept in the Lord"; or perchance some apostle, who, with his numerous band of missionaries, went forth to preach the Gospel to benighted nations.[1] The names, or native places of many foreigners, who flocked to the hives of learning and sanctity in Ireland, are noted in an especial manner. Here are found invoked the names of Italian, Egyptian, British, and Gallic saints, who had been buried in Ireland.[2]

Dr. Lanigan incorrectly asserts, that the foregoing work is sometimes called *Saltair-na-rann*, which means, the Metrical or Multipartite Psalter.[3] But it would appear from Colgan's

---

[1] See also Harris' *Ware*, vol. iii. *Writers of Ireland*, book i. chap. v. pp. 52, 53.

[2] The portion of this work, known as the Litany, has been translated and published for the first time in the *Irish Ecclesiastical Record*, vol. iii. Nos. xxxii. and xxxiii., for May and June, 1867. The original Irish occupies one side of the page, in the Irish characters ; while on the opposite side, there is a correct English translation, by a competent scholar, writing under the initials B. M. C. Explanatory notes are found at the foot of nearly all those pages. A learned dissertation precedes this Litany, taken from the Archives of St. Isidore's Franciscan Convent, at Rome. Some years ago, Dr. Todd examined this MS., containing ten *folia*, which he found to have constituted a part of the *Book of Leinster*. This fact would seem to identify it with the MS. seen at Louvain, and described by Father Soller, the Bollandist, as we have already stated. In point of antiquity, therefore, this version dates back to the first half of the twelfth century. These *folia* contain the Martyrology of Tallaght—to which allusion has been already made—together with five of seven works attributed to Ængus. Ward and Colgan consulted this MS.; for their readings seem to have been marked, and these are very useful in assisting the Irish scholar to decipher certain words. However legible in their time, these are nearly altogether defaced at present. In Ward's and Sirin's Acts of St. Rumold, published at Louvain in 1662, this Litany is quoted at great length, p. 206. With the exception of the groups of seven bishops, nearly all the saints, whose intercession is invoked, are given.

[3] *Ecclesiastical History of Ireland*, vol. iii. chap. xx. § x. p. 247. And in note (106, p. 251) he remarks on this passage: "Under this title Colgan says (*ib.*, p. 582) that it appears in some old Irish MSS. and that he got a part of it with the inscription, *from Saltair-na-rann composed by Aengus Cele-De.* He observes, that the latest saint mentioned in it is St. Tigernach, son of St. Mella, and founder of Doire-melle (see chap. xix. § 18), who died abbot of Kill-achad, in the now county of Cavan, on the 4th of November, A.D. 805 (806). See *AA. SS.* p. 796, and Archdall at *Killachad*). This is a strong proof of the assertion that Aengus was the author of this work".

statement, that the *Saltair-na-rann* was altogether a distinct work.[1] After describing the work, "De Sanctis Hiberniae", he mentions the *Saltair-na-rann* as having been composed in the Irish language; and, of course, as being distinct from the first named treatise, which had been written mostly in Latin. Yet, I must confess, that the sentences employed by Colgan in his account are rather ambiguous.[2] The work entitled " De Sanctis Hiberniae", does not appear to have been a metrical composition, as may be seen in extracts taken from it, and found in many of Colgan's notes. The *Saltair-na-rann* comprises a History of the Old Testament,[3] written in verse,[4] and which is attributed to Ængus as its author. We are informed, that the Chronicle of Ængus Ceilé De, known as *Saltair-na-Rann*, i.e. " Saltair of the Poems" or " Verses", has been so called, because, *Salm*, " Psalm", and a Poem are the same.[5] It contains one hundred and fifty poems, composed in the finest style of the Gaelic language, as understood in the eighth century.

This celebrated work of Aengus Ceilé De has been called

[1] There is a MS. Martyrology, entitled *Saltair-na-Rann*, preserved in the British Museum [Egerton, 185]. It is a thin, small quarto-sized volume in verse, and, with exception of a few pages, it has been written in the bold and accurate hand of Dubhaltach Mac Firbisigh, about the year 1650. It consists of sixty-seven pages, containing five quatrains, or twenty lines, on each page. The title is in accordance with the second quatrain, which, as Anglicised, thus begins:

" The Saltair of the verses shall be the name
Of my poem: it is not an unwise title".

This *Saltair-na-Rann*, however, is entirely distinct from that of Aengus Ceilé De.

[2] " Opus ex jam memoratis opusculis conflatum in quibusdam antiquis patriae membranis patrio sermone intitulatur Saltuir-na-rann: quae vox Latine reddita Psalterium metricum, nunc Psalterium multipartitum denotat. Et in utroque sensu, diversa S. Aengussii opera recte sic inscribi poterant". *Acta Sanctorum Hiberniae, xi. Martii. Vita S. Aengussii,* cap. xv. pp. 581, 582. I know not on what authority Harris makes the following statement with regard to Ængus, when he says, " to him is ascribed by some *Psalter-na-rann*, being a Miscellany Collection of Irish affairs, in prose and verse, *Latin* and *Irish*". Harris' *Ware*, vol. ii. *Writers of Ireland,* book i. p. 53.

[3] The other *Saltair-na-Rann*, to which allusion has been made in a preceding note, contains three hundred and twelve quatrains, written in the inferior Gaelic of the sixteenth, if not of a later century. Yet, it is not, strictly speaking, a Gaelic Martyrology; for all the Irish saints Professor O'Curry could discover in it were, St. Patrick, St. Brigid of Kildare, St. Ciaran of Saighir, and St. Ciaran of Clonmacnois. According to the poet's arrangement, every quatrain commenced with a saint's name, but sometimes there are three or even four quatrains devoted to one day, as the number of festivals happened to fall within it. Every saint, however, has a separate quatrain devoted to him. The modern writer, who supplied Mac Firbis's omissions, has admitted some incorrections. See *Lectures on the Manuscript Materials of Ancient Irish History,* Lect. xvii. pp. 360, 361, and *Appendix,* No. cix. p. 609.

[4] Harris says, this work had been written in *elegant metre,* but he seems to regard it as a distinct work from the *Psaltar-na-rann.*

[5] See *Rev. Dr. Keating's History of Ireland, Preface.* This writer adds that a *Salterium* and a *Duanaire,* or " book of poems", are identical.

Saltair-na-rann.[1] It is distributed into parts.[2] It has been written in the form of prayers, tending to raise the reader's mind to the love of God, and to the celebration of His praise, for all the Creator's works are referred to His greater glory, and rest upon His power as their final cause. The foregoing reasons are assigned by Colgan for this work deserving the title of *Saltair-na-rann.*[3] A different work, compiled from the five small treatises already mentioned, in which our saints are invoked, in the form of a prayer, might be well called *Psalterium multipartitum*, as Colgan remarks, on account of the various parts into which it is distributed. He adds, that both authority testifies and evidence persuades us, that it had been thus inscribed and composed by St Ængus. The authority assigned is that of an old parchment MS., from which the treatise, "Homonymi", already described, has been extracted. It was sent from Ireland[4] to Colgan. It bore the following title:

[1] This is most probably the work described by O'Reilly, where he says : "Aengus also wrote the *Psalter-na-rann*, which is an abridged history of the descendants of Abraham, from the birth of Isaac, until after the death of Moses". * * * * * * "The Psalter-na-rann is preserved in a large MS., the property of Sir William Betham. It is written in a fine strong hand, and occupies upwards of six folio pages, closely written on the largest size vellum". *Chronological Account of nearly Four Hundred Irish Writers*, p. liv.

[2] In Harris' *Ware*, vol. iii. (*Writers of Ireland*, book i. chap. v. p. 33), it is said that some ascribed to Aengus a *Psalter-na-rann*, being a miscellany on Irish affairs, in prose and verse, Latin and Irish. "Aengus wrote no such work", says Dr. Lanigan, "and his only *Psalter*, or *Saltair-na-rann*, were those above mentioned. Harris got his information either from Toland, or from some one who took it from him. In his *Nazarenus* (*Letter* ii. sect. 8) Toland says that Aengus wrote a *chronicle*, entitled *Psalter-na-rann*". This is characterized as a falsehood invented by an impious writer, who did not wish it to be known, that Aengus was chiefly employed in treating about saints, and that he used to invoke them. At chap. ii. § 8, Toland advances a still more monstrous statement, viz , that the Irish used not pray to saints. Now, nothing is more clear in our ecclesiastical history, than that our ancient Irish progenitors were in the habit of invoking them. Dungal, a most learned Irishman of the early times, defends this practice against Claudius. Brogan, who in the seventh century wrote St. Brigid's Life in Irish verse, often invokes her in the course of it, and concludes with these words: "There are two holy virgins in heaven, who may undertake my protection, Mary and St. Brigid, *on whose patronage let each of us depend*". To omit many other proofs, Adamnan, in his *Vita S. Columba*, lib. ii. cap. 45, bears testimony. This practice was so general in Ireland, and so well known to learned men, who have examined our history, that in his *Discourse on the Religion of the Ancient Irish*, Ussher found it expedient not to touch on invocation of the saints. See Dr. Lanigan's *Ecclesiastical History of Ireland*, vol. iii. chap. xx. § x. n. 107, p. 251.

[3] Colgan says : "Uti aptissime in utroque sensu Saltair-na-rann, i.e. Psalterium metricum, vel Psalterium multipartitum, vocari posset; uti et de facto in alterutro, vel utroque sensu nuncupari et intitulari consuevit". *Acta Sanctorum Hiberniae*, xi. *Martii. Vita S. Aengussii*, cap. xv. p. 582. The late Professor Eugene O'Curry told me, he had examined a magnificent copy of the *Psalter-na-Rann*, at Oxford. At that time, he informed the writer, no perfect copy of it was known to be extant in Ireland.

[4] The person who brought this book with him from Ireland was the Very

" Homonymi Hiberniae Sancti ex Saltair-na-rann, quod compo-suit Ængussius Keledeus". The *Saltair-na-rann* is interpreted by Colgan to mean the *Multipartite Psalter*. Reason, he says, induces us to believe that this had been a work of St Ængus, since there is no saint found in any portion of it, who had not departed life before the time of St. Ængus, or who had not been, at least, his cotemporary. This matter had been dis-covered, by a careful collation of this treatise with our annals and native records. According to these later authentic sources, no saint, mentioned in the work alluded to, is found to have lived after A.D. 800, except St. Tigernach, founder of Doire-melle monastery. He is said to have departed A.D. 805, at which time there can be no doubt that Ængus was still living. For, although our annals relate the death of St. Melditribius in the year 840, yet, it is doubtful, if he be the saint bearing that name, and mentioned in the fortieth chapter of the second book, as already described.[1]

There are Pedigrees of Irish saints yet existing, and these have been generally ascribed to Aengus Ceilé De. Several copies of this tract are preserved in our ancient MSS.; but it is doubtful, if any of these date back, in their present state, to the time of Aengus, towards the close of the eighth or beginning of the ninth century. In the copies we possess, there may be defections or additions, as compared with the original composition. The oldest copy known is also the best and most copious,[2] and its genuineness has been generally admitted by most of our anti-quarians. It is the more valuable, because it almost invariably

Rev. Father Francis Mathew, at one time Guardian of the Convent at Louvain, and Franciscan Provincial over the Irish province. He was a man of much erudition, austerity of life, and very zealous in the cause of religion. He presented this work, already mentioned, to Colgan, in the year 1633. By his preaching, exhortations, and pious labours, he had greatly contributed for many years to the advancement and preservation of Ireland's orthodox and persecuted faith. At length, having endured various trials and tortures, with the greatest patience and constancy, this pious sufferer was put to death by the Protestants, A D. 1643. Colgan adds, that Geoffrey Keating, also, in the second book of his History, attributes this work to St. Ængus. See Colgan's *Acta Sanctorum Hiberniae, xi. Martii*, n. 14, p. 583.

[1] See Colgan's *Acta Sanctorum Hiberniae, xi. Martii. Vita S. Ængussii*, cap. xv. p. 582. Colgan observes, that he was induced to treat, at some length, on the valuable works of this venerable saint, that his readers might know what great antiquity and authority attached to the aforesaid Martyro-logies and other works, and which he had so frequently taken occasion to quote in his own volumes. *Ibid.* It would also appear, Colgan intended to publish the works of St. Ængus, had his own life been prolonged. *Ibid.*, cap. xiv. p. 581.

[2] This is found in the Book of Leinster, which was compiled within the years 1120 and 1160. A copy is contained in the Book of Ballymote, compiled in 1391; and another in the Book of Lecain, written A.D. 1416. A later still is found in the great Book of Genealogies, compiled by Dudley Mac Firbis, in 1650.

gives references to the sites of churches, in connection with the holy persons whose pedigrees are found recorded. It often enumerates and traces the lineage of groups of persons or associates, who occupied these churches at one time, and occasionally their successors for a few generations. In the form of annotations, an immense amount of ecclesiastical and topographical information is conveyed. These historic comments establish with satisfactory exactness a date for the foundation of nearly all our primitive churches. It is an almost invariable rule with the venerable genealogist, to trace the pedigree of each saint to some remarkable personage, whose name and period can be ascertained from our national records and books of secular genealogy.[1]

This is the oldest collection of our national saints' pedigrees known to be in existence. Its exact time of composition cannot be determined, but it was probably one of Aengus's latest and most matured literary efforts.

VII.—*Modes of life at Tallagh until the time arrived for departure.—St. Ængus returns to Clonenagh, where he is chosen as Abbot.—Supposed to have been a Chorepiscopus.— Occasional retirement to Dysart Enos.—His death and burial. —Value of St. Ængus' hagiographical works.—Conclusion.*

We may well conceive how affectionately and agreeably passed their hours of occasional relaxation, as of study, while the holy Abbot Melruan and Aengus were companions, in the *coenobium* at Tallagh. Their interchange of pious and cultivated thought must have proved mutually conducive to the accuracy and unction of those hagiographical and sacred historic works, which seem specially to have had a literary fascination for them. The teaching of ecclesiastical and secular learning probably engaged a considerable part of their daily monastic routine. For we cannot doubt but native and foreign literature, as also the science of the period, was then taught in the school of Tallagh, with the religious training and dogma peculiar to such establishments. It seems evident, from references made to Eusebius and St. Jerome, that Aengus was well versed

---

[1] See Professor Eugene O'Curry's *Lectures on the Manuscript Materials of Ancient Irish History*, Lect. xvii. pp. 359, 360. This learned writer adds: "By referring to these pedigrees, you may easily find the time at which any of the early saints of Erinn flourished. As, for instance, St. *Colum Cille* is recorded to have been the son of *Feidlimidh*, son of Fergus, son of Conall, son of Niall "of the Nine Hostages", monarch of Erinn, who was killed in the year 405. Now, by allowing the usual average of thirty years to each of the four generations from Niall to Colum, making 120 years, and adding them to 405, we shall find that Colum (who is known to have died in the year 592) must have been born about the year 520. He was actually born, as we know from other sources, in 515".

in the Greek as in the Latin language. So long as Melruan lived, peace and security reigned within the Irish monastic enclosures. Had he survived a few years, the tocsin of alarm would have sounded the first approach of Northman invasions; while many of the shrines and illuminated Books of Erinn were destined to suffer wreck and ruin from the Pagan spoilers.

When holy Melruan had been called to bliss, our saint keenly felt the loss of his society and gentle rule. The sylvan shades around Tallagh had less attraction during the noon-tide walk, and more lonely seemed the solitudes of scarped ravines and mountains. Climbing topmost heights of the latter, the eyes of Aengus were often turned towards the rich plains beneath, through which the Liffey and Barrow flowed. Peering beyond their bounds, the hills of Dysart were seen on a distant south-western horizon. Old associations were revived; nor were the monastery and monks of Clonenagh forgotten in the train of awakened recollections. Perhaps some message from its superior and inmates urged his return. In prosecuting his archaic studies, Aengus had travelled to many places, and always with some holy and useful object in view. It now seemed the will of Heaven, that he should turn once more towards the land of Leix and Ossory; and, accordingly, we may suppose a sympathetic tear coursed down his cheeks and those of his fellow-religious, when he took scrip and staff, bidding adieu for the last time to those blissful haunts of science and religion, where he had spent some of his life's best years. We know not the exact period when he parted from this mountain home; but, it appears altogether likely, his renowned superior had departed this life before Aengus thought of leaving, nor had the eighth century drawn quite to its close.

Ængus survived his friend the holy Abbot of Tallaght for a very considerable period. The name of St. Molruan is found in his *Festilogium*, where he is called the "Bright Sun of Ireland".[1] This circumstance seems to prove, that his work, in its finished state, must have been composed subsequently to the year 792. After remaining some years at Tallaght, Ængus returned to Clonenagh His ascetic and literary fame must have culminated to a high degree, at the time his thoughts reverted to the old retreat:—

"Here to return and die at home at last".[2]

[1] A mistake, probably a typographical one, occurs in Dalton's *History of the County of Dublin*, p. 761, where the death of Saint Molruan, or Maelruan, is referred to the year 787, whereas the year 788 is named for the first arrival of Ængus at Tallaght. The real date for St. Molruan's death is the 7th day of July, 792. This accomplished and usually accurate historian incorrectly tells us, when giving the history of Tallaght, and speaking of Ængus, that he died "Abbot of this house in 824". *Ibid.*

[2] Oliver Goldsmith's *Traveller*.

Doubtless, he was welcomed by the good abbot and his community at Clonenagh.   Over this great monastery, in due course
he was chosen Abbot.   He is said to have succeeded Melathgenius, who died in 767 (*recte* 768), according to Ware.[1]
He was also elevated to the episcopal dignity ; for it was a very
usual practice then prevailng in Ireland, to invest the superiors
of all our great religious houses with this exalted rank.   But,
we may regard this dignity he obtained, as qualifying him to be
classed only with the inferior prelates, known as Chorepiscopi,
in early times.   Dr. Lanigan thinks it probable, that St. Ængus
had been Abbot over a monastery at Dysartenos, which he is
supposed to have founded, whilst he also presided over Clonenagh.[2]

But notwithstanding his elevation, and the duties that de-
volved upon him, in virtue of his high office, as Abbot over
the greater monastery, that favourite retreat at Dysartenos,[3]
seems to have been ever dear to his recollections.   Finding his
end approaching, Ængus withdrew to the scenes of his former

[1] It is not probable, however, that our saint was the immediate successor of
Melathgenius.   By his namesake, Ængus Ceilé De is called Abbot.   In the
Martyrologies cited in a succeeding note, it will be seen, that he was also
styled Bishop.

[2] Another Ængus, who was almost contemporary with this saint, has left
an elegant poem in praise of him.   From this poem Colgan derives a great
part of St. Aengus Ceilé De's *Acts*.   That the writer of this poem was abbot
at Clonenagh, as also at Disert-Aengus, is possible, and Colgan observes, that
his hints are even stronger as to the latter place.   The matter can easily be
settled.   As both places lay near each other, within the barony of Maryborough, Aengus might have been abbot over both these establishments.   Disert-
Aengus, which commenced with himself, may be considered simply as a cell
to the older and greater monastery at Clonenagh.   At *Clonenagh* and *Disert-
enos*, or *Disert-Aengus*, Archdall has inverted the order of Aengus' transactions.   After making Aengus found an abbey at Disert-Aengus, Archdall
sends him to Tallaght, where, it is said, he died.   Now, it is clear from the
Acts, that Aengus was no more than a simple monk when he removed to
Tallaght.   As to the place of his death, it could not have been Tallaght ; for,
as we find in said *Acts*, he was buried at Clonenagh.   That Aengus, who was
panegyrist of our saint, seems to have been, as Colgan justly conjectures,
abbot Aengus, surnamed the *Wise*.   He belonged to Clonfert-Molua, and died
in 858 or 859.   See Colgan, *A A. SS.* p. 582, and also Dr. Lanigan's *Ecclesiastical History of Ireland*, vol. iii. chap. xx. § x. n. 98, pp. 248, 249.   In a
succeeding note, Dr. Lanigan remarks : " Considering the Irish practice of
promoting eminent abbots to the episcopacy, we need not look for any other
see for him than one of the above mentioned monasteries".   *Ibid.*, n. 99,
p. 249.

[3] Mr. O'Donovan, in the Tenth Article of his edited *Miscellany of the Irish
Archaeological Society*, vol. i. note g., comments on the term Disert, a common
topographical prefix to Irish localities.   He says :—" This word, which is
translated *desertus locus* in " Cormac's Glossary", and *desertum* by Colgan
(*Acta Sanctorum*, p. 579), is sometimes used in ancient Irish manuscripts, to
denote a hermitage, or an asylum for pilgrims or penitents.   It occurs in this
latter sense in the *Leabhar Braec*, fol. 100, a. a., and in the Book of Leinster,
in the MS. Library of Trinity College, Dublin, H. 2, 12, fol. 118, b. a".—*Irish
Charters in the Book of Kells*, n. (g.) p. 112.

retirement and austerities. He breathed his last prayers with his last breath, about the year 824, according to the most probable conjecture, on Friday, the 11th day of March.[1] Sir James Ware names one or other of the years 819, 824, or 830, conjecturally, as referring to our saint's death, from the circumstance of the 11th March falling on the *feria sexta*, or Friday, at each of these dates. Professor Eugene O'Curry thinks St. Aengus Ceilé De must have died about the year 815.[2] We know not how many years he lived; but probably this saint had not attained a very advanced age, when his death occurred.

Ængus was buried at Clonenagh, according to his Acts, as given by Colgan.[3] But, whether he died there or at Dysartenos is uncertain.[4] If he built a monastery at the latter place, no trace of its ruins can be discovered at present;[5] and hence, it might be a safe conjecture to suppose Dysartenos had been only a cell or hermitage, constructed by St. Ængus, for his sole accommodation and retirement.[6]

---

[1] " There being good reason to think that Aengus survived the year 806, Colgan conjectures that the year of his death was either 819, 824, or 830; whereas in each of them the 11th of March fell on a Friday". Dr. Lanigan's *Ecclesiastical History of Ireland*, vol. iii. chap. xx. § x. n. 100. p. 249. "Ita eodem die Martyrologium Tamlact. *Aengussii Episcopi Hoblenii nepotis.* Marian. *Magnus Aengussius Hoblenii nepos Episcopus.* Mart. Dungall. *Aengussius nepos Hoblenii, Episcopus, est qui composuit festilogium.* In ipso etiam Aengussii Festilogio in quibusdam exemplaribus ponitur nata hac die: sed illa insulsa additio est: quae idcirco in vetustioribus exemplaribus non reperitur". Colgan's *Acta Sanctorum Hiberniae, xi. Martii,* n. 15, p. 583.

[2] See *Lectures on the Manuscript Materials of Ancient Irish History,* Lect. xvii. p. 362.

[3] See *Acta Sanctorum Hiberniae, xi. Martii, Vita S. Aengussii,* cap, xvi. p. 582.

[4] In the note already given, the anonymous scholiast says, that our saint was both educated and buried at Disert-Aengus. It is certain, however, that Aengus had been educated at Clonenagh. Colgan remarks, that the Disert named, either is not different from Clonenagh, or our saint most probably died and had been buried at the first place, his body having been afterwards translated and deposited at Clonenagh. But, he acknowledges that our annals make a distinction between both places, as in reality they were bound to do. A distance of some miles intervenes between Dysartenos and Clonenagh. The present writer is fully cognizant of this fact, and has long been conversant with the bearing and local peculiarities of both places.

[5] Alluding to this locality of Dysartenos, however, a writer well knowing its folk-lore observes: " Not many years ago, the remains of the foundation of St. Aengus's sacred edifice were discovered by a farmer, who professed the doctrines of the Church of England. This farmer, much to his credit, reverentially would not suffer the remains to be disturbed. He re-covered with earth the stone steps that rested at the foot of the once altar, on which the holy anchoret offered the Sacrifice of the Mass. The field in which this discovery was made is near to the dwelling of Mr. James Lawler". O'Byrne's *History of the Queen's County,* chap, xxi. p. 57.

[6] In what part of Dysartenos parish this cell, or monastery, if such, was situated, the antiquary is not likely to discover. Many remains of old buildings are yet standing in the immediate neighbourhood. If, however, I might be allowed to offer a conjecture, St. Aengus possibly selected for his cell the

It is indeed very certain—as a distinguished Irish scholar and most devoted Catholic[1] well observes—that St. Aengus Ceilé De[2] cannot be set down for an ignorant nor a superstitious monk; but, on the contrary, he must ever be regarded as a gifted writer, deeply read in the Holy Scriptures, and in the civil and ecclesiastical history of the world. He was especially versed in that historic lore contained in what he calls enthusiastically " The Host of the Books of Erinn". Taking the Festology of St. Aengus as a purely historic tract, largely interwoven with the early civil and ecclesiastical history of Ireland, there is probably no European country which possesses so early a national document and one of a character so important. A great number of the primitive Christian inhabitants and strangers, in our island, have been introduced by name into this valuable treatise. Their festival days, with copious references to the early denominations and exact situations of our old churches and monasteries, severally founded by many of them, are accurately given; and already, by means of this tract, if not all, at least nearly all, of these foundations may be or have been identified, by competent archaeologists. His other writings are hardly less valuable for their historic, national, and religious interest.

The truly learned are ever truly humble. But to raise this latter qualification to the degree of heroic virtue requires a special intervention of the spirit of wisdom. Towards our saint, God's choicest graces appear to have been vouchsafed. From his early years, he was gifted with a docile mind, an ardent love of true perfection, humility of disposition, an understanding capable of comprehending a wide circle of science,

site on which the former Protestant church of Dysart may now be seen, as a comparatively modern ruin. When Sir Charles Coote wrote his *Statistical Survey of the Queen's County*, in 1801, he describes Dysart church, as standing " on one of the lofty hills of the same name, with a square tower or steeple, which has a very picturesque appearance". Chap. ix. § iv. p. 117. An ancient graveyard is to be found there, even yet much resorted to for the interment of deceased Catholics. No doubt, the very old parish church occupied this site. From or near this elevated position, the ruins of Clonenagh's " seven churches" are clearly visible under favouring circumstances.

[1] See Professor Eugene O'Curry's *Lectures on the Manuscript Materials of Ancient Irish History*, Lect. xvii., p. 870.

[2] In a contribution to the *Gentleman's Magazine* for the month of July, 1865, the following remarks may be found, on the Irish term céíle vé, Anglicised *Culdee*. It is " used by our annalists to denote a monk or friar, even at a comparatively modern period of our history. In O'Donovan's *Annals of the Four Masters*, at the year 1595, we find an application of such term to the Dominicans in Sligo monastery. The reader, who desires the fullest accumulated testimonies and learned investigation, in reference to the Culdees, will examine the researchful contribution of the Rev. William Reeves, in *Transactions of the Royal Irish Academy*, vol. xxiv. It has since been published as a separate tract, entitled, *The Culdees of the British Islands, as they appear in History, with an Appendix of Evidences;* Dublin. 1864".

human and divine, with an imagination, fervid, brilliant, chaste, and correct, as ever gifted a poet.   Our Church and country have received no inconsiderable services from the literary labours and learning of this saint, while his life had been beautifully and edifyingly consistent with his teaching and acquirements. Some men possess dazzling qualities and acquire renown in this world, while their minds and dispositions are cold, vitiated, and corrupt; they may shine among their fellow-mortals, as the skin of the venomous snake or crawling reptile appears radiant with variegated colours, under the rays of a bright sun.   On the contrary, in solitude and retirement, wishing to avoid the applause or rewards of the world, under a rude garb and exterior, our saint, like the glow-worm, luminous even through the darkness of night, has diffused a steady and an undiminished light over the obscurity of our scattered ecclesiastical records and traditions, in his own time and for preceding ages.   He has likewise transmitted to us some of the most venerable remains of our ancient aud holy literature, so long and so providentially preserved in Ireland and in more distant countries. Let us hope, that under the careful editorship of a competent Irish scholar, these fragments will be gathered ere they perish, that they will be committed to type, published, and thus rendered accessible to the generality of readers.   While such documents serve to excite and sustain our religious feelings, they also fan the spirit of patriotism, and serve to extend still more the real fame of our beloved country.   The holy Aengus Ceilé De laboured wisely and well in his generation.   He has left to this day and to all succeeding generations, the heritage of his zeal, his learning, his genius, his virtues, and his noble example.

THE END.

J. F. Fowler, Steam Press Printer, 3 Crow Street, Dame Street, Dublin.